The North American Fourth Edition

CAMBRIDGE LATIN COURSE

UNIT 2

Stage Tests

The North American Cambridge Classics Project
Test Booklet Committee

Stephanie M. Pope, Chair
Norfolk Academy, Norfolk, Virginia

Virginia M. Blasi
Shore Regional High School, West Long Branch, New Jersey

Richard M. Popeck
Stuarts Draft High School, Stuarts Draft, Virginia

Dorothy M. Rossi
Monroe Middle School, Rochester, New York

Publications Officer, NACCP

Richard M. Popeck

CAMBRIDGE
UNIVERSITY PRESS

PUBLISHED BY THE PRESS SYNDICATE OF THE UNIVERSITY OF CAMBRIDGE
40 West 20th Street, New York, NY 10011-4211, USA

The Cambridge Latin Course was funded and developed by the University of Cambridge School Classics Project and SCDC Publications, London, and is published with the sponsorship of the School Curriculum Development Committee in London and the North American Cambridge Classics Project. The work of the School Curriculum Development Committee has now been taken over by the Qualifications and Curriculum Authority.

First published 1999
This edition 2001

Printed in the United States of America

ISBN 0 521 00510 8

Table of Contents

Preface

At the 1992 annual meeting of the North American Cambridge Classics Project, an idea arose that there should be machine scoreable tests for the *Cambridge Latin Course*. Virginia Blasi, Stephanie Pope, Richard Popeck, and Dorothy Rossi volunteered to be on the committee, and Stephanie Pope was selected as the chair. After sifting through numerous tests submitted by teachers and settling on the basic format, headings, and directions, these machine scoreable tests were produced and field tested for four years. Student comments were taken very seriously, and appropriate changes were made. These tests represent the writers' best efforts to produce tests for all types of schools, all types of students, and all types of educational philosophies. While the Committee realizes that no test is perfect, these pages represent a sincere and concerted effort by Cambridge Latin teachers to produce tests that accurately and fairly test the content of each stage of Unit 2 of the *Cambridge Latin Course*.

The following people have generously allowed their work to be included in this edition: Elaine Batting (MA), Pat Bell (ONT), Mary Jane Bickley (TX), Virginia Blasi (NJ), Carlene Craib (MA), Carol Ellis (TX), Fran Kirschner (NJ), Ellen Lamb (NY), Stephanie Pope (VA), Richard Popeck (VA), Helen Richards (TX), Dorothy Rossi (NY), Mary Shults (NY), and Marlene Weiner (NJ). Stan Farrow's NACCP publication – *Fabulae Ancillantes* – was the source for several stories used in these tests. The stories used for Stages 18, 19, and 20 came from the North American Fourth Edition Unit 2 Teacher's Manual for the *Cambridge Latin Course*. The drawings found on the tests came from the textbooks and workbooks of the North American Fourth Edition of the *Cambridge Latin Course*. Great thanks are owed to the students and faculty of the various schools who so patiently endured the inevitable typos and so sincerely made the helpful suggestions that have allowed these tests to become useful for students of all grade levels.

Stephanie M. Pope
Norfolk Academy
Norfolk, Virginia

Introduction

Teachers who adopt the *Cambridge Latin Course* as their basal text often feel overwhelmed by the amount of material and the number of stories they must cover in each Stage. It is difficult to learn all the new stories, to produce grammar / culture worksheets, and to write tests all at the same time. This booklet is designed to aid teachers who are new to the reading comprehension approach and to provide the veteran Cambridge teachers with a standardized set of tests that reflect the two major objectives of the *Cambridge Latin Course*: "to teach comprehension of the Latin language through practice in reading it" and "to develop the students' understanding of the social and political history of the Romans, especially during the first century A.D."

As a result, each test starts with a reading passage that pertains to the context of the Stage just finished. As with the textbook, a *Words and Phrases Checklist* is provided for the terms not met in the captioned line drawings that start each Stage and the *Vocabulary Checklists* that complete each Stage. Following the reading passages are comprehension and grammar questions appropriate for the content of that Stage or previous Stages.

The remainder of the test consists of a variety of sections designed to evaluate the student's knowledge of grammar, vocabulary, derivatives, and culture. Often students are asked to demonstrate their understanding through the manipulation of grammar points presented in the tested Stage. The grammar terms used on the test are those actually mentioned in the Stage text or in the Language Information found at the end of each textbook. All grammar questions are based upon the information presented in the text and delineated in the teacher's manual.

There will always be a derivative section where students must select an English word that most closely defines a Latin derivative used in an English sentence. Occasionally students are asked to match the derivative to the Latin word from which it is derived or to its actual English definition. The derivative sections contain words based on the Latin words found in that Stage's *Vocabulary Checklist*.

Several culture sections are interspersed throughout the test to provide variety and, perhaps, a break from some of the more demanding comprehension and grammar sections.

Each test has the same format. There are 100 machine scoreable items. For schools that do not have Scantron machines, a blank Student Answer Sheet is supplied so that the tests may be graded by the more traditional method. In addition, every effort has been made to standardize these tests. For instance, the headings and directions are the same for every recurring section so that students will not become confused by instructions that change with every test. Each test contains drawings from the textbook in an effort to appeal to learners of all types. While macrons were omitted from all of the Latin sections to comply with the format students must face on the National Latin Exam, the SAT II Tests, and the Advanced Placement Examinations, they may appear when an answer to a grammar question depends upon them.

Though abbreviations were avoided at all costs, space restrictions required the use of some of them. Listed below are the abbreviations used in this booklet:

sing. = singular	nom. = nominative	pres. = present
pl. = plural	acc. = accusative	impf. = imperfect
masc. = masculine	dat. = dative	perf. = perfect
fem. = feminine	abl. = ablative	plupf. = pluperfect

Each test was designed to be taken within a forty-four minute period.

This Committee realizes that each teacher may want to emphasize different items. Teachers should feel free to adapt the tests to fit their courses or their district's requirements.

Many members of this Committee feel **strongly** that these exercises should be viewed as standardized tests and must **never** be given to students to keep. The tests may be used by students and teachers for practice and review, but the physical test should be retained by the teachers as there are currently no plans to produce more tests for Unit 2 in the near future.

After five years of careful review, the NACCP Test Booklet Committee is pleased to present *Cambridge Latin Course* teachers with these tests which, it sincerely hopes, will prove to be helpful for every teaching situation.

Stage 13 Test

**PLEASE DO NOT WRITE ON THE TEST BOOKLET.
MARK ALL ANSWERS ON THE ANSWER SHEET.**

I   Directions

Read the story and answer the following comprehension questions.

"ego," inquit Bregans, "in culina manere volo. Varica me quaerit, quod	1
taurus horreum novum **delevit**. ego taurum ducebam. tamen **neglegens**	2
eram. taurus fugit et **impetum** in hoc aedificium fecit. quod neglegens	3
eram, nunc Varica est iratus.... ego tecum cenam parare possum! placetne	4
tibi?"	5
"mihi non placet!" clamavit Volubilis. "ego sum coquus **peritus**	6
Aegyptius; tu es servus ignavus Britannicus. abi! **hic** manere non potes."	7
Bregans, postquam e culina **invitus** exiit, Varicam conspexit. **vilicus**	8
multis cum servis horreum **reficiebat**. vilicus servique, quod diligenter	9
laborabant, Bregantem non viderunt. **ille** igitur **post** villam cucurrit, ubi	10
nemo eum videre **poterat**.	11
subito Loquax et Anti-Loquax e villa venerunt. gemini Bregantem	12
salutaverunt.	13
"salve, Bregans! cur tu horreum non reficis?"	14
"vilicus me ad villam misit," respondit Bregans. "ego servis cibum	15
fero."	16
"cur nullum cibum habes?" rogavit Loquax.	17
"Volubilis **occupatus** est," respondit Bregans. "**necesse est** mihi hic	18
manere."	19

Words and Phrases

taurus - bull
delevit - destroyed
neglegens - careless
impetum - charge
peritus - skillful
Aegyptius - Egyptian
hic - here
invitus - unwilling

vilicus - manager
reficiebat - was repairing
ille - he
post - behind
nemo - no one
poterat - was able
occupatus - busy
necesse est - it is necessary

1. **To whom does Bregans make his statement at the beginning of the paragraph?**
   a. dominus
   b. vilicus
   c. coquus

2. **Who is searching for Bregans?**
   a. dominus
   b. vilicus
   c. coquus

3. **Whom does Bregans blame for his current problem?**
   a. himself
   b. Varica
   c. the bull

4. **Why is Varica angry?**
   a. Bregans fell asleep.
   b. Bregans knocked over a new granary.
   c. Bregans let a bull run free which in turn destroyed the new granary.

5. **What happened after Bregans left the kitchen?**
   a. Varica saw him.
   b. He spied Varica and the other slaves repairing the granary.
   c. Varica and the other slaves saw him.

6. **Where did Bregans go?**
   a. behind the house
   b. in front of the house
   c. inside the house

7. **What were Loquax and Anti-Loquax doing when Bregans ran into them?**
   a. leaving the house
   b. repairing the granary
   c. doing nothing

8. **What reason did Bregans give to the twins for not helping the rest of the slaves?**
   a. Salvius ordered him to the house.
   b. Varica ordered him to the house.
   c. Volubilis ordered him to the house.

9. **From this story what can we say about Bregans? He is_____.**
   a. an obedient slave
   b. a hard worker
   c. a good liar

                                        Stage 13

II Directions

Identify the following grammar/structure items based on the content of the story.

10. **In line 1 <u>manere</u> is used as a(n) _____.**
    a. direct object
    b. complementary infinitive
    c. object of a special verb

11. **In line 2 the tense of <u>delevit</u> is _____.**
    a. present
    b. imperfect
    c. perfect

12. **In line 3 the tense of <u>eram</u> is _____.**
    a. present
    b. imperfect
    c. perfect

13. **In line 4 the tense of <u>est</u> is _____.**
    a. present
    b. imperfect
    c. perfect

14. **In line 4 -<u>ne</u> in <u>placetne</u> is _____.**
    a. a verb ending
    b. a question sign
    c. a noun ending

15. **In line 5 <u>tibi</u> is used as a(n) _____.**
    a. direct object
    b. complementary infinitive
    c. object of a special verb

III Directions

Match the Latin definition to the characters from Stage 13.

16. Alator   a. canem ingentem curat.

17. Anti-Loquax   b. Salvium vulneravit.

18. Bregans   c. aratoribus praeest (is in charge of).

19. Cervix   d. optime saltare potest.

20. Loquax   e. suaviter cantare potest.

21. Philus	a. villam et servos curat.
22. Rufilla	b. servum aegrum interficere vult.
23. Salvius	c. numerare potest.
24. Varica	d. cenam optimam coquere potest.
25. Volubilis	e. multas ancillas habet.

IV Directions

Select the verb that correctly translates the <u>underlined</u> word(s).

26. **Your letter <u>has arrived</u>.**
    a. advenit
    b. adveniebat
    c. advēnit
    d. advenire

27. **Father <u>used to say</u> that all the time.**
    a. dicit
    b. dicebat
    c. dixit
    d. dicere

28. **We are able <u>to run</u> to your house.**
    a. currimus
    b. currebamus
    c. cucurrimus
    d. currere

29. **<u>We were singing</u> in the rain.**
    a. cantamus
    b. cantabamus
    c. cantavimus
    d. cantare

30. **<u>Are you keeping</u> your receipts, Leroy?**
    a. retines
    b. retinuisti
    c. retinebas
    d. retinere

                                        Stage 13

V Directions

Match the Latin Word to its antonym/opposite.

31. advenit   a. cupit

32. non vult   b. discedit

33. ita vero   c. minime

34. decidit   d. dat

35. retinet   e. surgit

VI Directions

Answer the following based on your knowledge of Vocabulary Checklist words.

36. Which Latin word comes **closest** in meaning to *ruere* ?
    a. festinare   b. decidere   c. iacere   d. capere

37. Which Latin word is **closest** in meaning to *interficere* ?
    a. incidere   b. credere   c. legere   d. necare

38. Based on underline{meaning}, which Latin word does **NOT** belong?
    a. villa   b. aedificium   c. vita   d. horreum

39. Which Latin word describes an **emotion**?
    a. laetus   b. aeger   c. fessus   d. nullus

40. Which word does **NOT** describe a verbal action?
    a. dicere   b. trahere   c. nuntiare   d. narrare

VII Directions

Tell the conjugation to which each verb belongs.

41. advenio, advenire, adveni   a. first   b. second   c. third   d. fourth

42. numero, numerare, numeravi   a. first   b. second   c. third   d. fourth

43. decido, decidere, decidi   a. first   b. second   c. third   d. fourth

44. retineo, retinēre, retinui   a. first   b. second   c. third   d. fourth

45. interficio, interficere, interfeci   a. first   b. second   c. third   d. fourth

VIII Directions

Identify the character from our stories who said the following.

46. ____ inquit, "servus aeger est inutilis. ego servos inutiles retinere nolo."
    a. Pompeius   b. Salvius   c. Bregans   d. Varica

47. ____ inquit, "rex Cogidubnus, amicus tuus, tibi canem dedit."
    a. Pompeius   b. Salvius   c. Bregans   d. Varica

48. ____ inquit, "hi servi aratoribus cibum ferunt. placetne tibi?"
    a. Cervix   b. Anti-Loquax   c. Salvius   d. Varica

49. ____ inquit, "omnes Britanni sunt stulti, sed iste Bregans est stultior quam ceteri!"
    a. Anti-Loquax   b. Cervix   c. Salvius   d. Pompeius

50. ____ inquit, "ubi est vinum? ego aquam bibere non possum!"
    a. Anti-Loquax   b. Bregans   c. Varica   d. Volubilis

     Stage 13

IX Directions

Select the verb that correctly completes the sentence.

51. **ego pugnare ____.** a. possum b. potes c. possumus d. possunt

52. **tu leonem necare ____.** a. non vis b. non vult c. non vultis d. nolunt

53. **puer laborare ____.** a. nolo b. non vult c. nolumus d. nolunt

54. **vos vinum bibere ____.** a. volo b. vis c. volumus d. vultis

55. **viri cantare ____.** a. potes b. potest c. possumus d. possunt

56. **nos vinum bibere ____.** a. volo b. vis c. volumus d. vultis

X Directions

Match the meaning to the derivative of __dicere__.

57. predict   a. assert the opposite

58. contradict   b. a habitual inclination

59. valediction   c. foretell

60. addiction   d. a decision, judgment

61. verdict   e. a farewell

XI Directions

Select the correct answer for each of the following culture questions.

62. ____ was the first Roman to lead his troops into Britain.
    a. Julius Caesar   b. Augustus Caesar   c. Claudius

63. This man first led Roman troops into Britain in ____.
    a. 55 B.C.   b. 44 B.C.   c. A.D. 84

64. The first Roman emperor was ____.
    a. Julius Caesar   b. Tiberius Caesar   c. Augustus Caesar

65. The Roman who ordered the invasion of Britain in A.D. 43 was ____.
    a. Claudius   b. Julius Agricola   c. Augustus Caesar

66. Why did this person order the invasion of Britain?
    a. The Britons had attacked Rome.
    b. He needed a military success.
    c. He needed a new supply of slaves.

67. When Britain became a Roman province, its first governor was ____.
    a. Aulus Plautius   b. Julius Agricola   c. Tiberius Claudius

68. At the time of our stories, the governor of Britain was ____.
    a. Julius Agricola   b. Aulus Plautius   c. Tiberius Claudius

69. The Romans built roads in Britain for the use of ____.
    a. merchants   b. farmers   c. soldiers

70. The Romans remained in Britain for approximately ____ years.
    a. 7   b. 250   c. 400

71. A temple commemorating Claudius' invasion of Britain was built at ____.
    a. Londinium   b. Camulodunum   c. Noviomagus

XII Directions

Match the meaning to the Latin verb form.

72. poteras

    a. to be able

73. potuisti

    b. you used to be able

74. potes

    c. you had been able

75. posse

    d. you could

    e. you can

****

76. estis

    a. you are

77. eratis

    b. you have been

78. fuistis

    c. you will be

79. esse

    d. you used to be

    e. to be

****

80. nolunt

    a. they did not want

81. nolle

    b. they had not wanted

82. noluerunt

    c. they do not want

    d. not to want

XIII Directions

Indicate whether the following culture statements are true or false by marking **a** *for* **true** *and* **b** *for* **false.**

83. Under Roman rule, the Britons had to obey Roman law and pay Roman taxes.

84. Agricola wanted to provide the Britons with the comforts of civilization.

85. Some British tribes resisted the Roman invasion.

86. The Arval Brotherhood performed religious ceremonies and prayed for the Emperor.

87. Salvius had little or no military experience.

88. The Druids were in charge of Celtic religion.

89. The Romans were tolerant of Celtic gods and religion.

90. After being defeated at Mons Graupius, the Romans retreated from Scotland.

91. The Roman conquest of Britain provided economic benefits to British potters and metalworkers.

XIV Directions

Choose the correct form to replace the <u>underlined</u> form.

92. **Salvius <u>milites et centurionem</u> salutavit.**
    a. milites centurionemque
    b. militesque centurionem

93. **Varica <u>servos et ancillas</u> inspexit.**
    a. servosque ancillas
    b. servos ancillasque

XV Directions

Select the word(s) which most closely define(s) the <u>underlined</u> derivative.

94. **Grumio was a <u>novice</u> at the art of deception.**
    a. old-timer   b. expert   c. newcomer   d. patron

95. **Salvius <u>enumerated</u> Bregans' shortcomings.**
    a. demonstrated   b. forgot about   c. criticized   d. counted

96. **He offered to help us of his own <u>volition</u>.**
    a. wealth   c. choice
    b. disregard   d. religious beliefs

97. **The <u>alternative</u> was not pleasant.**
    a. change   b. second choice   c. third choice   d. result

98. **The daredevil rider was in a <u>vulnerable</u> position as his motorcycle jumped the cars.**
    a. victorious   b. harmful   c. safe   d. viewing

99. **The <u>advent</u> of the comet was an astronomical wonder.**
    a. arrival   b. departure   c. viewing   d. tail

100. **Good <u>diction</u> is important in Latin class.**
    a. reading ability   b. speaking ability   c. writing ability   d. spelling

Stage 14 Test

**PLEASE DO NOT WRITE ON THE TEST BOOKLET.
MARK ALL ANSWERS ON THE ANSWER SHEET.**

I   Directions

Read the story and answer the following comprehension questions.

Salvius in tablino stabat. iratissimus erat, quod Philum exspectabat. **1**
epistulam dictare volebat. tandem Philus tablinum **lente** intravit. servus **2**
fasciam latam gerebat. **3**

"epistulam scribere non possum," inquit, "quod **bracchium** meum est **4**
fractum. Bregans sellam in ianua **reliquit**. ego sellam non vidi et ... ." **5**

"caudex!" clamavit Salvius. "servus **laesus** est **inutilis**. ego ... ." **6**

subito Rufilla in tablinum festinavit. "mi Salvi," clamavit uxor. **7**
"Volubilis, coquus noster, cenam parare non potest. Bregans **fenestram** **8**
aperuit, ubi **pluebat**. nunc Volubilis cibum coquere non potest, quod **9**
carbo madidus est. Anti-Loquax, ubi hanc aquam **verrere temptabat,** ad **10**
terram decidit. nunc pedem fractum habet et saltare non potest." **11**

"quid?" clamavit Salvius attonitus. "num Bregans totam **familiam** **12**
delevit? iste servus stultissimus est." **13**

tum dominus Loquacem conspexit. **14**

"Loquax!" clamavit. "tu pedem fractum non habes. **fortasse** tu totam **15**
rem narrare potes. quid **accidit**?" **16**

Loquax tamen non respondit, quod nihil dicere poterat. **guttur** **17**
tumidum habuit! **18**

Words and Phrases

lente - slowly
fasciam - bandage
latam - wide
gerebat - was wearing
bracchium - arm
fractum - broken
reliquit - left
laesus - injured
inutilis - useless
fenestram - window

aperuit - opened
pluebat - was raining
carbo - charcoal
madidus - wet
verrere - to sweep up
temptabat - was trying
familiam - household
fortasse - perhaps
accidit - happened
guttur tumidum - laryngitis

---

1. **Why was Salvius so angry?**
   a. He had hurt himself.
   b. He could not find a stilus.
   c. Philus was late.

2. **Why can't the letter be written?**
   a. Philus has a broken arm.
   b. Salvius has a broken arm.
   c. Bregans has a broken arm.

3. **What was Salvius' response to the statement in lines 4–5?**
   a. concern
   b. impatience
   c. sympathy

4. **What is Rufilla's complaint?**
   a. She has a broken foot.
   b. Bregans broke a window.
   c. Volubilis can't cook dinner.

5. **What will Salvius now lack?**
   a. food for dinner
   b. his wife
   c. a broken foot

6. **What was Volubilis' problem?**
   a. a broken foot
   b. a broken arm
   c. wet charcoal

7. **Whom does Salvius characterize as very stupid?**
   a. Philus   b. Bregans   c. Anti-Loquax

8. **What does Salvius hope that Loquax can do for him?**
   a. make dinner   b. destroy the family   c. tell him the truth

9. **What did Loquax do?**
   a. told him everything   b. could not talk   c. gave Salvius laryngitis

10. **What one thing did Bregans <u>not</u> do?**
    a. leave the window open in a rain storm
    b. put a chair in a doorway
    c. fall on the wet floor

II Directions

Identify the following grammar/structure items based on the content of the story.

11. **In line 1 <u>iratissimus</u> is a _____ adjective.**
    a. positive
    b. comparative
    c. superlative

12. **In line 1 <u>Philum</u> is the _____ .**
    a. subject   b. direct object   c. indirect object

13. **In line 2 <u>dictare</u> is a(n) _____ .**
    a. infinitive   b. direct object   c. prepositional phrase

14. **In line 5 <u>sellam</u> is used as a(n) _____ .**
    a. subject   b. direct object   c. indirect object

15. **In line 9 <u>pluebat</u> is in the _____ tense.**
    a. present   b. imperfect   c. perfect

16. **In line 12 <u>num</u> is the type of question that expects a _____ .**
    a. positive reply   b. negative reply   c. yes/no reply

17. **In line 13 <u>delevit</u> is in the _____ tense.**
    a. present   b. imperfect   c. perfect

18. **In line 15 <u>habes</u> is in the _____ tense.**
    a. present   b. imperfect   c. perfect

19. **In line 17 <u>poterat</u> is in the _____ tense.**
    a. present   b. imperfect   c. perfect

20. **In lines 17–18 <u>guttur tumidum</u> are in the _____ case.**
    a. nominative   b. accusative   c. dative

III Directions

Select the word(s) that most closely define(s) the <u>underlined</u> derivative.

21. **The <u>regicide</u> surprised the subjects – the killing of the _____ .**
    a. prince   b. princess   c. queen   d. king

© QCA Enterprises Limited 2001   Stage 14

22. **The jeweler gave an <u>appraisal</u> of the ring.**
    a. estimated value   c. count of carats
    b. heritage   d. cleaning

23. **The program focused on <u>quotidian</u> problems.**
    a. numerous   c. daily
    b. few   d. reporting

24. **The editor <u>deleted</u> an entire page.**
    a. added   b. took out   c. rewrote   d. praised

25. **The Romans used to <u>deify</u> their emperors.**
    a. praise them   b. bury them   c. curse them   d. make them into gods

26. **The <u>difficulty</u> of climbing a mountain is finding sure footing.**
    a. trouble   b. ease   c. fun   d. interest

27. **The students exhibited <u>fidelity</u> to their former club.**
    a. opposition   b. loyalty   c. financial support   d. disinterest

28. **We like to <u>donate</u> to Operation Smile.**
    a. help   b. participate   c. give   d. make posters for

29. **<u>Marital</u> problems are increasing these days – problems pertaining to _____ .**
    a. the sea   c. female horses
    b. marriage   d. the exploration of the planet Mars

30. **I was <u>astonished</u> by the color of my student's hair.**
    a. pleased   c. amazed
    b. saddened   d. scared

IV   Directions

Tell whether the following prepositions take the ablative or accusative case. Use **a** *for* **accusative,** **b** *for* **ablative,** *or* **c** *for* **accusative or ablative**.

31. per   34. cum   37. pro

32. de   35. ab   38. apud

33. in   36. prope

V Directions

Pick the form of the Latin word which correctly translates each sentence.

39. **We wanted to hear about the slaves.**
    nos de _____ audire voluimus.
    a. servum   b. servos   c. servis   d. servo

40. **Loquax ran through the house.**
    Loquax per _____ cucurrit.
    a. villa   b. villis   c. villas   d. villam

41. **Quintus rushes to the palace.**
    Quintus ad _____ ruit.
    a. aula   b. aulas   c. aulis   d. aulam

42. **Rufilla wanted to live in the city.**
    Rufilla in _____ habitare volebat.
    a. urbes   b. urbem   c. urbe   d. urbibus

43. **Volubilis wanted to stay at Varica's house.**
    Volubilis apud _____ manere voluit.
    a. Varicam   b. Varicas   c. Varicis   d. Varica

44. **Domitilla walked away from the merchants.**
    Domitilla a _____ ambulavit.
    a. mercatore   b. mercatorem   c. mercatores   d. mercatoribus

45. **Philus hurried into the kitchen.**
    Philus in _____ contendit.
    a. culinas   b. culinis   c. culinam   d. culina

VI Directions

*Indicate whether the following culture statements are true or false by marking **a** for **true** and **b** for **false**.*

46. A source of running water was a major consideration for an owner when choosing a site for a villa in Britain.

47. Each villa in Roman Britain produced everything it needed to sustain itself.

48. Domestic slaves led an easier life than slaves who worked the land.

49. The son of a skilled slave would have been able to learn his father's trade at a very early age.

50. Sugar was used to sweeten food in Roman Britain.

VII Directions

Using your knowledge of life in Roman Britain and this picture, select the answers for the following questions.

51. **From where did the family of the house get water for their animals?**

    a. the impluvium

    b. the ocean

    c. a well

52. **How did the farmer's wife sweeten the family's boiled cereal?**

    a. with sugar

    b. with honey

    c. with maple syrup

53. **What animals pulled the farmer's plow?**

    a. pigs

    b. horses

    c. oxen

54. **What is one way in which <u>this</u> British house is similar to a Pompeian house of a wealthy citizen?**

    a. heating system

    b. a compluvium

    c. a lararium

55. **What grain crops might the farmer have grown in the field he is plowing?**

    a. wheat

    b. rice

    c. soybeans

VIII Directions

Indicate whether the following grammar statements are true or false by marking **a** *for* **true** *and* **b** *for* **false.**

56. A Latin adjective agrees with a noun in person, number, and gender.

57. Adjectives indicating size or quantity usually come before the noun that they describe.

58. Latin adjectives always have the same endings as the nouns they modify.

59. Nouns and adjectives are grouped by their conjugation number.

60. The word **number** indicates whether nouns and adjectives are singular or plural.

IX Directions

Select the answers that most correctly complete the following culture statements.

61. ___ , complete with a <u>tepidarium</u> and <u>caldarium</u>, could be found in an elaborate villa.
    - a. Shrines
    - b. Workshops
    - c. Amphitheaters
    - d. Baths

62. **Romans brought _____ to Britain.**
    - a. oranges
    - b. watermelon
    - c. kiwi fruit
    - d. cherries

63. **Archaeologists have found traces of these crops in ___.**
    - a. cooking utensils
    - b. bones of skeletons
    - c. storage jars
    - d. the earth

64. **A simple farm tool would be a _____.**
    - a. sickle
    - b. strigil
    - c. stilus
    - d. gladius

65. **Farming tools in Roman Britain were made of iron and ___.**
    - a. wood
    - b. stone
    - c. bone
    - d. bronze

66. **Bees were kept __.**
    - a. as pets
    - b. as a status symbol
    - c. to protect property
    - d. as a source of honey

67. **Grain was harvested with ___.**
    - a. tractors
    - b. reapers
    - c. sickles
    - d. hoes

68. **Most of Salvius' ___ slaves would have been British.**
    - a. farm
    - b. household
    - c. mine working
    - d. gladiatorial

69. **In theory, any owner who killed a sick slave could be ___.**
    - a. excused from punishment
    - b. fined by the governor
    - c. charged with mistreatment of property
    - d. charged with murder

X Directions

Select the correct translation for <u>quam</u> *and* <u>quamquam</u> *in the following sentences.*
Answers may be used more than once.

70. Britanni <u>quam</u> ferocissime pugnaverunt.

71. puer est laetior <u>quam</u> puella.

72. <u>quam</u> pulchra est puella!

73. puer <u>quam</u> celerrime cucurrit.

74. cubiculum est elegantius <u>quam</u> tablinum.

75. <u>quamquam</u> puer erat pulcher, non erat fidelis.

a. although

b. as ____ as possible

c. how

d. than

XI Directions

Select the adjective that correctly completes the sentence.

76. _____ pueri amphoram portare non possunt.
    The small boys are not able to carry the amphora.
    a. parvus   c. parvi
    b. parvum   d. parvos

77. tres servos _____ in fundo videmus.
    We see the three lazy slaves on the farm.
    a. ignavus   c. ignavos
    b. ignavum   d. ignava

78. Bregans tres _____ amphoras spectat.
    Bregans looks at the three huge amphoras.
    a. ingentem   c. ingentibus
    b. ingentes   d. ingenti

79. Salvius quinque servos ___ habet.
    Salvius has five loyal slaves.
    a. fidelis   c. fideles
    b. fidelem   d. fidelibus

80. Bregans _____ canes videre non potest.
    Bregans is not able to see the large dogs.
    a. magnus   c. magni
    b. magnum   d. magnos

XII Directions

Match the definition to the character described.

81. Domitilla   a. Salvium et Rufillam visitabat.

82. Marcia   b. cubiculum Quinto ornavit.

83. Quintus   c. in Campania militabat.

84. Salvius   d. anus et ancilla erat.

85. Rufilla   e. ignavissima ancilla erat.

XIII Directions

Select the adjective which correctly completes the sentence.

86. ____ **servi sunt iuvenes**.
    Many slaves are young men.
    a. multi   b. multae   c. multus   d. multa

87. **"uxor," Salvius inquit, "es ____ !"**
    Salvius said, "Wife, you are crazy!"
    a. insanus   b. insanae   c. insana   d. insani

88. **venator ____ bestias agitabat**.
    The hunter was chasing the larger beasts.
    a. maior   b. maiores   c. maiorem   d. maiori

89. **familiaris est vir ____ .**
    My relative is a sophisticated man.
    a. urbanos   b. urbanis   c. urbanum   d. urbanus

90. **"Britanni," inquit Salvius, "sunt ____ ."**
    a. stultissimos   b. stultissimus   c. stultissimis   d. stultissimi

91. **Salvius agricolas ____ vituperavit**.
    a. bonos   b. bonas   c. bonam   d. bonum

XIV Directions

Select the answer which best translates the Latin sentence.

92. **num pecuniam e tablino extraxisti?**
    a. Did you take the money from the study?
    b. Surely you didn't take the money from the study, did you?
    c. Surely you took the money from the study, didn't you?
    d. You took the money from the study?

93. **Volubilis ad culinam revenit cibumque paravit.**
    a. Volubilis returned the food to the kitchen and was preparing it.
    b. Volubilis returned the food and prepared it in the kitchen.
    c. Volubilis returned and prepared the food in the kitchen.
    d. Volubilis returned to the kitchen and prepared the food.

94. **salutavitne iucunde Quintum Salvius?**
    a. Did Salvius greet Quintus pleasantly?
    b. Surely Salvius greeted Quintus pleasantly?
    c. Salvius greeted Quintus.
    d. Surely Salvius didn't greet Quintus pleasantly?

XV Directions

Select the picture of the slave(s) who would have had a higher status in Salvius' household.

95.

A.  B.

96.
A.   B.

97.
A.   B.

98.
A.   B.

XVI Directions

Follow the directions for the statements based on these pictures.

A.   B.   C.

99.   Select the picture that shows the **<u>uxor</u>**.

100.   Select the picture that shows the **<u>maritus.</u>**

Stage 15 Test

PLEASE DO NOT WRITE ON THE TEST BOOKLET.
MARK ALL ANSWERS ON THE ANSWER SHEET.

I Directions

Read the story.

olim mercator diem natalem celebrabat. mercator Caecilium ad cenam	1
invitavit. Caecilius cum servo ad villam contendit, ubi mercator	2
habitabat. servus erat Phormio. Caecilius, postquam villam intravit,	3
multos amicos vidit. cena amicos valde delectavit. omnes multum vinum	4
bibebant et multas fabulas narrabant. tandem e villa discesserunt.	5
Caecilius et Phormio quoque discesserunt. viae erant **desertae**, quod	6
omnes Pompeiani dormiebant.	7
tres fures tamen per vias **errabant**. fures, postquam Caecilium	8
conspexerunt, dixerunt:	9
"ecce! Caecilius adest. Caecilius est argentarius et multam pecuniam	10
habet."	11
fures Caecilium ferociter pulsabant; Caecilium ad terram **deiecerunt**.	12
Phormio tamen ad fures **se praecipitavit** et omnes superavit. Caecilius,	13
postquam **convaluit**, Phormionem **liberavit**. Caecilius Phormioni	14
multam pecuniam dedit, quod fidelis erat.	15

Words and Phrases

desertae - deserted
errabant - were wandering
deiecerunt - threw

se praecipitavit - cast himself headlong
convaluit - recovered
liberavit - set free

II   Directions

Indicate whether the following comprehension statements are true or false by marking **a** *for* **true** *and* **b** *for* **false**.

1. A merchant celebrated his birthday.

2. Caecilius went alone to a house.

3. Caecilius did not know many of the people at the party.

4. Everyone enjoyed the food.

5. They had slaves to entertain them.

6. The streets were deserted because the Pompeian citizens were drinking wine.

7. Thieves were wandering through the streets.

8. In lines 10–11 the thieves recognized Caecilius.

9. The thieves attacked Caecilius because he was a merchant.

10. Caecilius beat these people ferociously.

11. The thieves threw Caecilius to the ground.

12. Phormio overpowered the thieves.

13. Caecilius set Phormio free once Phormio had recovered from his wounds.

14. Phormio gave Caecilius money.

15. Caecilius appreciated the fact that Phormio was loyal.

III   Directions

Identify the following grammar/structure items based on the content of the story.

16. **In line 1 <u>celebrabat</u> is in the _____ tense.**
    a. present   b. imperfect   c. perfect

17. **In line 3 <u>erat</u> is in the _____ tense.**
    a. present   b. imperfect   c. perfect

                                    Stage 15

18. **In line 4 valde is a(n) _____.**
    a. adverb   b. adjective   c. noun

19. **In line 5 fabulas is used as a(n) _____.**
    a. object of a preposition   b. subject   c. direct object

20. **In line 6 discesserunt is in the _____ tense.**
    a. present   b. imperfect   c. perfect

21. **In line 6 desertae is used as a _____.**
    a. subject   b. predicate adjective   c. predicate nominative

22. **In lines 10–11 the subject of habet is _____.**
    a. pecuniam   b. argentarius   c. Caecilius

23. **In line 12 the subject of deiecerunt is _____.**
    a. fures   b. Caecilium   c. terram

24. **In line 14 Phormioni is used as a(n) _____.**
    a. direct object   b. indirect object   c. object of a special verb

25. **In line 15 fidelis is a _____ adjective.**
    a. positive   b. comparative   c. superlative

IV Directions

Select the word(s) that most closely define(s) the <u>underlined</u> derivative.

26. **She always felt claustrophobic in elevators. She had the fear of ____.**
    a. heights   b. speed   c. enclosure   d. people

27. **He did not let the snow storm impede his progress.**
    a. frighten   b. slow   c. hasten   d. lighten

28. **We never understood how he acquired the fracture.**
    a. wart   b. broken bone   c. bruise   d. scratch

29. **A nautical theme was selected for the banquet.**
    a. cowboy   b. naval   c. urban   d. beach

30. **The fort was in a tenable position.**
    a. defendable   b. open   c. camouflaged   d. lucky

31. **The town began to <u>undulate</u> with the movement of the volcanic magma.**
    a. rise and fall   b. burn   c. moan   d. crack

32. **The criminal was convicted of a <u>prior</u> offense.**
    a. later   b. serious   c. previous   d. malicious

33. **He couldn't believe that he really saw a <u>saxifrage</u>.**
    a. heart-breaker   b. rock-breaker   c. home-breaker   d. law-breaker

34. **Some people thought that Talos was <u>invincible</u>.**
    a. defiant   c. unable to be conquered
    b. enterprising   d. reliant

35. **The <u>effigy</u> of Caecilius was beautiful.**
    a. good-luck charm   b. poem   c. inscription   d. image

V   Directions

Complete the following sentences by selecting the correct form of the noun.

36. **multae feminae cum _____ sedebant.**
    Many women were sitting with the chieftains.
    a. princeps   b. principes   c. principi   d. principibus

37. **turba prope _____ stabat.**
    The crowd was standing near the doors.
    a. ianua   b. ianuae   c. ianuas   d. ianuis

38. **principes ad _____ processerunt.**
    The chieftains proceeded to the pyre.
    a. rogum   b. rogo   c. rogis   d. rogus

39. **Britanni e _____ effigiem portaverunt.**
    The Britons carried the statue from the villa.
    a. villae   b. villa   c. villam   d. villarum

40. **in _____ erant multi principes.**
    In the house there were many chieftains.
    a. villae   b. villa   c. villam   d. villarum

VI Directions

*Indicate whether the following culture statements are true or false by marking **a** for **true** and **b** for **false**.*

41. A client king ruled on behalf of another, more powerful ruler.

42. A **colonia** was a town with farm allotments for Roman veterans.

43. The stone slab tells us that the temple in Noviomagus was dedicated to Neptune and Venus.

44. Cogidubnus was allowed to add two of the emperor's names to his own.

45. Cogidubnus probably received Fishbourne palace for the help he had given to Emperor Claudius.

46. Cogidubnus was granted the privilege of Roman citizenship.

47. The new temple in Noviomagus was a sign and a reminder of Roman power.

48. The Romans encouraged respect and worship of the emperor to build up a sense of unity in their large empire.

49. Noviomagus became the new capital town of the Regnenses.

50. A **collegium** was an association of British chiefs.

51. Cogidubnus' official title, which he received from the Romans, was client king.

VII Directions

Select the form of the adjective which agrees with the noun.

52. ____ **puer Cogidubnum ad effigiem duxit.**
    a. parva   b. parvum   c. parvus   d. parvam

53. **sacerdotes erant** ____ .
    a. paratae   b. paratas   c. paratos   d. parati

54. **sacerdotes effigiem _____ portabant.**
    a. ceratum   c. ceratas
    b. ceratos   d. ceratam

55. **Britanni _____ Cogidubnum visitabant.**
    a. nobilis   c. nobiles
    b. nobili   d. nobilibus

56. **nautae _____ ad Britanniam navigaverunt.**
    a. Romanus   b. Romana   c. Romani   d. Romanae

VIII Directions

Select the correct translation of quod. Mark **a** *for* **because** *or* **b** *for* **which**.

57. puer senem ducebat, **quod** claudicabat.

58. vinum, **quod** ancillae ferebant, erat in patera aurea.

59. facile est nobis vincere, **quod** nos sumus fortiores.

60. donum, **quod** regem maxime delectavit, erat equus.

IX Directions

Select the word to which the relative pronoun refers.

61. **femina, quam ego vidi, erat pulcherrima.**
    a. ego   b. pulcherrima   c. quam   d. femina

62. **navis crocea, quam Dumnorix navigabat, metae appropinquavit.**
    a. Dumnorix   b. quam   c. metae   d. navis

63. **erant multi viri, qui Romanos fortes impediebant.**
    a. qui   b. viri   c. Romanos   d. fortes

64. **amicus noster, quem nos exspectamus, aliam rotam quaerit.**
    a. amicus   b. rotam   c. nos   d. quem

65. **uxor, quae post Salvium ambulabat, flores portabat.**
    a. flores   b. quae   c. uxor   d. Salvium

Select the relative pronoun that correctly completes the sentence.

66. **rhetor, _____ pueros docet, est Graecus servus.**
    a. qui   b. quae   c. quod

67. **sculptor statuam, _____ est pulchra, facit.**
    a. qui   b. quae   c. quod

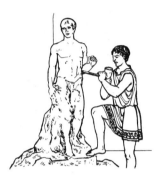

68. **ancilla, _____ urnam portabat, lente ambulabat.**
    a. qui   b. quae   c. quod

69. **plaustrum, _____ fractas rotas habet, est in via.**
    a. qui   b. quae   c. quod

70. **agnus, _____ servus ducebat, erat victima.**
    a. quem   b. quam   c. quod

XI Directions

amici *or* inimici? *Mark* **a** *if the person or tribe were friendly to the Romans when they invaded Britain, mark* **b** *if they opposed the Romans.*

71. Cartimandua

72. Durotriges

73. Caratacus

74. Iceni

75. Brigantes

76. Atrebates

77. Boudica

XII Directions

Match the Stage 15 Vocabulary Checklist word to its antonym/opposite.

78. laeta   a. mare

79. terra   b. misera

80. celeriter   c. fracta

                              d. nauta

                              e. lente

XIII Directions

Match the Stage 15 Vocabulary Checklist word to the word which means nearly the same.

81. superare
82. statua
83. redire

a. saxum
b. effigies
c. revenire
d. tenere
e. vincere

XIV Directions

*If the statement is **true** mark **a**, if the statement is **false**, mark **b**.*

84. The discovery of the Fishbourne palace was the result of an intensive search by British archaeologists.

85. Prasutagus left his lands to the Roman emperor Nero.

86. The Romans regarded a strong woman ruler as dangerous.

87. In Roman society, a wealthy Roman woman had the same rights and power that a wealthy British woman had in British society.

88. The Romans believed that Neptune was the god of the sea.

XV Directions

Answer the following questions based on the content of the stories in Stage 15.

89. Romani Britannos facile superaverunt, ubi Romani ad Britanniam venerunt.
    a. verum   b. falsum

90. omnes Britanni Romanis valde resistebant, ubi Romani ad Britanniam venerunt.
    a. verum   b. falsum

91. praecursores ambulaverunt post Salvium.
    a. verum   b. falsum

92. nulli Britanni ad caerimoniam ambulaverunt.
    a. verum   b. falsum

93. rex Cogidubnus ipse multas victimas sacrificavit.
   a. verum   b. falsum

****

94. Quintus donum ad aulam ferebat; donum erat _____ .
   a. urna   b. unguentum   c. flores   d. tripodas

95. flammae _____ consumebant.
   a. Claudium   b. aulam   c. effigiem   d. aquilam

96. _____ saepe in ludis funebribus vincebant.
   a. Atrebates   b. Brigantes   c. Regnenses   d. Cantiaci

97. _____ nautis, qui in certamine navali vicerunt, praeerat.
   a. Vespasianus   b. Belimicus   c. Dumnorix   d. Cartimandua

****

98. _____ inquit, "dei Claudium arcessunt."
   a. Cogidubnus   b. Salvius   c. Quintus   d. Vespasianus

99. _____ inquit, "non decorum est Britannis cives Romanos impedire."
   a. Salvius   b. Varica   c. Quintus   d. Cogidubnus

100. _____ inquit, "hi Regnenses sunt timidi; facile est nobis vincere!"
   a. Dumnorix   b. Belimicus   c. Cogidubnus   d. Boudica

Stage 16 Test

PLEASE DO NOT WRITE ON THE TEST BOOKLET.
MARK ALL ANSWERS ON THE ANSWER SHEET.

I Directions

Read the story and answer the following comprehension questions.

Bregans somnians

Cervix in fundo laborabat. subito Bregantem, qui in plaustro dormiebat,	1
conspexit. Cervix servum excitavit et clamavit,	2
"quam stultus es! **periculosum** est tibi in plaustro dormire. Salvius	3
semper servos ignavos ferocissime punit."	4
"eheu!" respondit Bregans. "ego miserrimus sum, quod de patre et	5
fratribus meis **somniabam**."	6
"ubi sunt pater fratresque tui?" rogavit Cervix.	7
"mortui sunt," respondit Bregans. "Romani eos interfecerunt."	8
tum Cervici rem totam narravit:	9
"ego et familiares mei sumus Iceni. **regina** nostra erat Boudica, quam	10
Romani saepe **vexabant**. tandem Boudica Icenos aliosque Britannos	11
vocavit. Iceni cum Romanis pugnaverunt. **primo** dei Icenis faverunt. Iceni	12
multos Romanos interfecerunt et urbes Romanas deleverunt. Suetonius	13
Paulinus, qui Britanniae praeerat, tandem **milites** Romanos **contra Icenos**	14
duxit. Iceni Romanis fortiter **resistebant**, sed Romani eos superaverunt.	15
inter mortuos erant pater fratresque mei.	16
"post pugnam milites Romani ad **vicum** nostrum venerunt, quod omnes	17
Icenos punire volebant. viros feminasque interfecerunt et vicum	18
deleverunt. me, qui tum puer eram, non necaverunt sed ad urbem	19
duxerunt. venalicio me vendiderunt. eheu! melius est mihi cum patre	20
fratribusque meis perire."	21
"quam misera est vita nostra!" inquit Cervix. "Romani ferocissimi sunt.	22
non Britanni, sed Romani sunt barbari."	23

Words and Phrases

somnians - dreaming	**primo** - at first
periculosum - dangerous	**milites** - soldiers
somniabam - was dreaming	**contra Icenos** - against the Iceni
regina - queen	**resistebant** - were resisting
vexabant - were treating badly	**vicum** - village

1. **Where did Cervix find Bregans?**
   a. on the farm   b. in the granary   c. in a wagon

2. **What did Cervix do then?**
   a. He woke up.   b. He shouted.   c. He fell asleep.

3. **What was Cervix's warning?**
   a. Salvius may punish you.   b. Salvius is lazy.   c. Salvius is stupid.

4. **About whom had Bregans been dreaming?**
   a. himself   b. his father and brothers   c. his mother and brothers

5. **Into which tribe had Bregans been born?**
   a. Cervici   b. Romani   c. Iceni

6. **Why did the tribal Queen Boudica lead a coalition of Britons in rebellion against the Romans?**
   a. She liked to treat the Romans badly.
   b. She liked to treat the Iceni badly.
   c. The Romans treated her badly.

7. **Why was the rebellion successful at first?**
   a. The Romans fought against many British tribes.
   b. The British fought among themselves.
   c. The gods seemed to favor the Iceni.

8. **What did the rebels achieve?**
   a. The Iceni killed many Romans.
   b. The Romans killed many Iceni.
   c. The Romans destroyed many towns.

9. **Who commanded the Roman army?**
   a. Agricola   b. Claudius   c. Paulinus

10. **How was his victory over Boudica achieved?**
    a. without any effort   b. after some resistance   c. quickly

11. **What did the Romans do in Bregans' village?**
    a. They killed the women and children.
    b. They captured the men and women.
    c. They killed the men and women.

12. **What happened to Bregans?**
    a. They tried to kill him.   b. They sold him.   c. They bought him.

13. **What did Bregans wish had happened? He wished _____ .**
    a. that he had died
    b. that he had escaped with his father and brothers
    c. that he had saved his father and brothers

14. **What did Cervix describe the Romans as being?**
    a. fierce   b. rather fierce   c. very fierce

15. **What is Cervix's general conclusion?**
    a. The Romans are the barbarians.
    b. The British are the barbarians.
    c. The British are the most fierce.

II   Directions

Identify the following grammar/structure items based on the content of the story.

16. **In line 1 <u>laborabat</u> is an example of the _____ tense.**
    a. imperfect   b. perfect   c. pluperfect

17. **In line 3 the translation of <u>quam</u> is _____.**
    a. than   b. as ___ as possible   c. how

18. **In line 4 <u>ferocissime</u> is an example of a _____ adverb.**
    a. positive   b. comparative   c. superlative

19. **In line 7 <u>fratresque</u> _____.**
    a. contains a replacement for <u>et</u>
    b. indicates a yes/no question
    c. indicates a question expecting a *no* answer

20. **In line 17 the best translation for <u>quod</u> is _____.**
    a. which   b. whom   c. because

21. **In line 18 the tense of <u>interfecerunt</u> is _____.**
    a. imperfect   b. perfect   c. pluperfect

22. **In line 20 <u>venalicio</u> is used as a(n) _____.**
    a. direct object   b. subject   c. indirect object

23. **In line 20 <u>mihi</u> is an example of a(n) _____ case.**
    a. nominative   b. dative   c. accusative

III Directions

*Select the correct translation for the **boldface** words.*

24. discipuli, cur **consentitis**?
    - a. do you agree
    - b. had you agreed
    - c. did you agree
    - d. were you agreeing

25. cur tu columbam **deridebas**?
    - a. are you mocking
    - b. did you mock
    - c. had you mocked
    - d. were you mocking

26. pueri in undis **perierunt**.
    - a. are dying
    - b. were dying
    - c. have died
    - d. had died

27. in mensa pocula **posuerant**.
    - a. are putting
    - b. were putting
    - c. have put
    - d. had put

28. ad urbem Athenas **effugerunt**.
    - a. flee
    - b. used to flee
    - c. fled
    - d. had fled

29. libertos **dimiserant** servi.
    - a. send away
    - b. have sent away
    - c. used to send away
    - d. had sent away

30. ubi **aedificavistisne** vias?
    - a. do you build
    - b. did you build
    - c. were you building
    - d. had you built

IV Directions

Select the answer that most correctly completes the sentence.

31. **Vespasian was a general who campaigned against the _____.**
    - a. Iceni
    - b. Atrebates
    - c. Durotriges
    - d. Cantiaci

32. **Fishbourne was originally the site of _____.**
    - a. a military depot
    - b. a temple to Neptune
    - c. a rebellion against the Romans
    - d. Boudica's tomb

33. **Fishbourne was a residence possibly built by _____.**
    - a. Claudius
    - b. Cogidubnus
    - c. Vespasian
    - d. Domitian

34. **Flowers along the paths of Fishbourne could have been _____, a Roman favorite.**
    - a. chrysanthemums
    - b. violets
    - c. roses
    - d. azaleas

35. _____ stood along the paths at Fishbourne, due to underground pipes.

    a. Hypocausts   b. Statues   c. Mosaics   d. Fountains

36. **Fishbourne was laid out in wings around a central _____ .**

    a. garden   b. peristylium   c. statue   d. atrium

37. **Craftsmen were brought from _____ to work on the palace.**

    a. Greece   b. Egypt   c. France   d. Italy

38. **Fishbourne palace, as we know it, was begun in _____ .**

    a. 45 B.C.   b. A.D. 45   c. A.D. 75   d. A.D. 125

V   Directions

Match the antonym/opposite to the Vocabulary Checklist word.

39. superesse   a. accipere

40. dimittere   b. num

41. consentire   c. postridie

42. nonne   d. dissentire

                      e. perire

VI   Directions

*Indicate whether the following culture and story statements are true or false by marking **a** for* **true** *and **b** for* **false.**

43. After the boat race, Belimicus was mocked even by slaves.

44. After he left Egypt, Quintus visited Greece.

45. Salvius was pleased by the entertainment offered by Cogidubnus.

46. The challenge of handling the bear did not intimidate Dumnorix.

47. Dumnorix threw a spear to try and save the king from the angry bear.

48. Quintus left Italy alone and sailed across the Mediterranean.

49. Cogidubnus provided the Romans with scouts and grain.

50. The opposition offered by the Durotriges to the Romans was easily overcome.

Directions

Select the relative pronoun that correctly completes the sentence.

51. fabri, _____ rex vehementer laudabat, aulam aedificaverant.
    a. qui   b. quem   c. quod   d. quos

52. rex iuvenem, _____ fabros servavit, ad aulam invitavit.
    a. qui   b. quem   c. quod   d. quos

53. servi ursam, _____ celeriter eos petivit, terruerunt.
    a. quod   b. quem   c. quam   d. quae

54. saltatrix saxum, _____ secum tulerat, tenebat.
    a. quod   b. quem   c. quam   d. quae

55. mensa, _____ servi paraverant, erat pulchra.
    a. quod   b. quem   c. quam   d. quae

VIII Directions

Match the definition to the person.

56. Belimicus   a. sought revenge because of naval defeat.

57. Clemens   b. stood and watched when the king was threatened.

58. Dumnorix   c. survived the disaster at Pompeii.

59. Germanicus   d. tried to save the king's life, but failed.

60. Salvius   e. looked after the "ursa ingens."

IX Directions

Identify the speakers of the following from our stories.

61. _____ inquit, "Romanis exploratores dedi."
    a. Quintus   b. Salvius   c. Belimicus   d. Dumnorix   e. Cogidubnus

62. _____ inquit, "facile est mihi ursam superare, homuncule."
    a. Quintus   b. Salvius   c. Belimicus   d. Dumnorix   e. Cogidubnus

63. _____ inquit, "servum qui tam fortis fuerat liberavi."
    a. Quintus   b. Salvius   c. Belimicus   d. Dumnorix   e. Cogidubnus

64. ____ inquit, "decorum est mihi eum punire."

    a. Quintus   b. Salvius   c. Belimicus   d. Dumnorix   e. Cogidubnus

65. ____ inquit, "ursam quae saltat videre volo."

    a. Quintus   b. Salvius   c. Belimicus   d. Dumnorix   e. Cogidubnus

X Directions

Identify the tense of the following verbs.

a = present   **b = imperfect**   **c = perfect**   **d = pluperfect**

66. laudabant

67. aedificaverant

68. plaudit

69. invitavit

70. consumpsit

71. potuerant

72. dixerat

73. agitabat

74. plauserunt

75. poterat

XI Directions

Select the word(s) that most closely define(s) the <u>underlined</u> derivative.

76. **The teacher could not get a <u>consensus</u> from the class.**
    a. agreement   b. thought   c. chuckle   d. commitment

77. **The <u>auxiliary</u> troops came too late.**
    a. scout   b. support   c. veteran   d. recruit

78. **The heads of state agreed to a <u>summit</u> conference.**
    a. peace   b. full   c. planned   d. top level

79. **The student had an <u>aversion</u> to philosophical essays.**
    a. dislike of   b. like of   c. indifference   d. aptitude for

80. **The <u>interim</u> reports were late in coming.**
    a. beginning of marking period   c. end of marking period
    b. mid-marking period   d. end of exam

81. **The victim was suing for <u>punitive</u> damages.**
    a. personal   b. professional   c. legal   d. punishing

82. **The dessert was a <u>delectable</u> treat.**
    a. delightful   b. sour   c. fattening   d. unexpected

83. **The trip to <u>Florida</u> was long awaited. From its name we know that Florida is a state filled with _____ .**
    a. sunshine   b. oranges   c. flowers   d. beaches

84. **Don't <u>fabricate</u> another story.**
    a. tell   b. make up   c. laugh at   d. cry at

85. **The teacher tried to <u>ameliorate</u> the situation.**
    a. lessen   b. heighten   c. improve   d. enjoy

XII Directions

Select the English phrase that correctly translates the <u>underlined</u> Latin phrase.

86. **amicus, <u>quem hospites deridebant,</u> iocum intellexit.**
    a. who was mocking the guests
    b. because he was mocking the guests
    c. whom the guests were mocking
    d. who mocked the guests

87. **dominus servos laudavit, <u>quod bene laboraverunt.</u>**
    a. who worked well   c. because they worked well
    b. which worked well   d. which they worked well

88. **naves, <u>quas Quintus exspectavit,</u> in portu erant.**
    a. who waited for Quintus   c. because they waited for Quintus
    b. which Quintus waited for   d. because Quintus waited for them

89. **coqui, <u>quos rex amavit,</u> subito perierunt.**
    a. who liked the king   c. because they liked the king
    b. whom the king liked   d. because the king liked them

90. **hospes donum, <u>quod optime amavit,</u> accepit.**
    a. who liked it very much   c. because he liked it very much
    b. which he liked very much   d. because he was very much liked

91. **Rufilla ancillae multam pecuniam dedit: <u>quam fortunata erat!</u>**
    a. who was fortunate   c. because she was fortunate
    b. whose fortune it was   d. how fortunate she was

XIII Directions

Pick the form of the noun which makes the sentence correct.

92. **The slaves put a large egg onto the table.**
    servi magnum ovum in _____ posuerunt.
    a. mensa   b. mensae   c. mensam   d. mensarum

93. **Among the beasts was a bear which danced.**
inter _____ erat ursa quae saltat.

    a. bestiae   b. bestiis   c. bestiarum   d. bestias

94. **On the next day, Quintus was walking with the king.**
postridie Quintus cum _____ ambulabat.

    a. rege   b. regem   c. regi   d. rex

95. **The sailors were sitting on the boat.**
nautae in _____ sedebant.

    a. navem   b. nave   c. navi   d. navis

96. **Who found out about the shipwreck?**
quis de _____ cognovit?

    a. naufragium   b. naufragii   c. naufragio   d. naufragia

XIV Directions

Mark the choice which correctly translates the Latin sentence.

97. **tune ursam spectare vis?**
    a. Surely you want to look at the bear, don't you?
    b. Do you want to look at the bear?
    c. You don't want to look at the bear, do you?
    d. The bear wants to look at the tuna?
    e. You don't want the bear to look at you, do you?

98. **nonne Paulinus Britannos superare poterat?**
    a. The Britons are not able to overcome Paulinus, are they?
    b. Is Paulinus able to overcome the Britons?
    c. Surely Paulinus is able to overcome the Britons?
    d. Paulinus was not able to overcome the Britons?
    e. Paulinus was able to overcome the Britons, wasn't he?

99. **num ursa regem petivit?**
    a. Did the bear attack the king?
    b. The bear didn't attack the king, did it?
    c. Surely the king didn't head for the bear, did he?
    d. Surely the bear headed for the king?
    e. The king didn't attack the bear, did he?

100. **ubi, o ubi est ursa mea, Luci?**
    a. Where and when did my bear go there, Lucius?
    b. Where is my bear, Lucius? There?
    c. Where is Lucius and my bear?
    d. When, o when was my bear there, Lucius?
    e. Where, o where is my bear, Lucius?

Stage 17 Test

PLEASE DO NOT WRITE ON THE TEST BOOKLET.
MARK ALL ANSWERS ON THE ANSWER SHEET.

I Directions

Read the story and answer the following comprehension questions.

Quintus cum rege Cogidubno in aula dicebat: 1
"ubi in urbe Athenis habitabam, ad forum cotidie ire poteram. in foro   2
mercatores **mercem** vendebant, cives cum amicis conveniebant,   3
philosophi contentiones habebant. haec urbs igitur **turbulentissima** erat." 4

"principes Britannici quoque turbulentissimi sunt," respondit rex.   5
"Belimicus enim Dumnorixque semper inter se **certant**. iste Belimicus me   6
paene necavit, quod Dumnorigem punire voluit. num Graeci   7
turbulentiores sunt quam Britanni?"   8

Quintus, qui post impetum **ursae** regem servaverat, ridebat: 9
"Graeci sunt **periculosi** quod callidissimi sunt, Belimicus quod   10
stultissimus est."   11

Words and Phrases

mercem - merchandise
philosophi - philosophers
contentiones - arguments
turbulentissima - very rowdy
certant - compete
ursae - of the bear
periculosi - dangerous

1. **Where was Quintus having this discussion?**
    a. in Greece   b. in Egypt   c. in Britain

2. **What city was he describing in the second paragraph?**
    a. Alexandria   b. Athenae   c. Noviomagus

3. **How often did Quintus go to the forum?**
    a. sometimes   b. every day   c. never

4. **How many collective groups of people were found in the forum?**

   a. 2   b. 3   c. 4

5. **How does he describe the city he visited?**

   a. rowdy   b. rather rowdy   c. very rowdy

6. **To whom does Cogidubnus compare Belimicus and Dumnorix?**

   a. merchants   b. citizens   c. philosophers

7. **In lines 7–8, what answer did Cogidubnus expect?**

   a. No, the Greeks aren't more rowdy.
   b. Yes, the Greeks are more rowdy.
   c. No, the Britons are not more rowdy.

8. **Quintus characterizes the Greeks and Belimicus as dangerous.**

   a. True   b. False

9. **Quintus thinks that Belimicus is very stubborn.**

   a. True   b. False

10. **According to Quintus, the Greeks are dangerous because they are very stupid.**

    a. True   b. False

II   Directions

Identify the following grammar/structure items based on the content of the story.

11. **In line 2 <u>cotidie</u> is a(n) _____ .**

    a. noun   b. adjective   c. verb   d. adverb

12. **In line 2 <u>poteram</u> is in the _____ tense.**

    a. present   b. imperfect   c. perfect   d. pluperfect

13. **In line 4 <u>turbulentissima</u> is a(n) _____ adjective.**

    a. positive   b. comparative   c. superlative   d. irregular

14. **In line 7 <u>voluit</u> is in the _____ tense.**

    a. present   b. imperfect   c. perfect   d. pluperfect

15. **In line 8 <u>Britanni</u> is in the _____ case.**

    a. nominative   b. accusative   c. dative   d. genitive

16. **In line 9 <u>ursae</u> is in the _____ case.**

    a. nominative   b. genitive   c. dative   d. accusative

17. **In line 9 <u>servaverat</u> is in the _____ tense.**
    a. present   b. imperfect   c. perfect   d. pluperfect

18. **In line 10 <u>sunt</u> is in the _____ tense.**
    a. present   b. imperfect   c. perfect   d. pluperfect

III Directions

Select the word(s) that most closely define(s) the <u>underlined</u> derivative.

19. **Baucis was truly a <u>magnanimous</u> person.**
    a. prejudiced   b. kindhearted   c. wonderful   d. optimistic

20. **The <u>gravity</u> of the situation was immediately recognizable.**
    a. levity   b. happiness   c. excitement   d. seriousness

21. **<u>Benign</u> strangers visited Baucis and Philemon.**
    a. large   b. kind   c. evil   d. foreign

22. **The clerk labored with <u>facility</u>.**
    a. enthusiasm   b. indifference   c. ease   d. anger

23. **There was a <u>paucity</u> of boys at the party.**
    a. multitude   b. crowd   c. small number   d. collection

24. **The players were <u>exanimate</u> after their loss.**
    a. enthusiastic   b. tired   c. interviewed   d. spiritless

25. **Originally <u>sincere</u> indicated that something was made _____ wax.**
    a. without   b. by casting in   c. out of   d. with a duplicate in

26. **In a literal sense, an <u>adherant</u> _____.**
    a. hears what others around him/her are saying
    b. is always here when she/he is needed
    c. sticks to his/her friends
    d. eavesdrops on others' conversations

27. **In a literal sense, an <u>insolent</u> person _____.**
    a. does not have the sunniest disposition
    b. does not like to be alone for long periods of time
    c. prefers to spend long periods of time alone
    d. acts in a manner uncustomary to what is expected

28. **In a literal sense, a <u>peninsula</u> is _____.**
   a. a small writing instrument
   b. a colony for writers
   c. almost an island
   d. insulated from the rest

IV Directions

Indicate whether the following culture statements are true or false by marking **a** *for* **true** *and* **b** *for* **false.**

29. Alexander the Great selected the site for the city of Alexandria.

30. Ptolemy succeeded Alexander as ruler of Egypt.

31. At the time of our stories, Alexandria was as large as Rome.

32. Alexandria's importance was due to its nearness to Greece.

33. The most visible part of Alexandria was the Pharos.

34. Ancient Alexandria had three harbors.

35. Canopus was the name of Alexandria's main street.

36. The Caesareum was a temple built for Julius Caesar by Cleopatra.

37. Alexander lived to see the city of Alexandria completed.

38. Alexander began the construction of the Pharos.

V Directions

Identify these places on the map by selecting the letter of the place that corresponds with its number on the map.

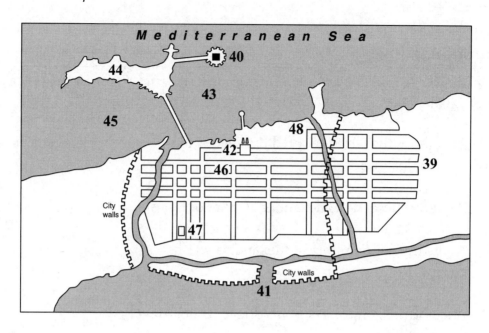

39.	a. Caesareum	44.	a. Museum
40.	b. Canopus Street	45.	b. Pharos Island
41.	c. Great Harbor	46.	c. Royal Quarter
42.	d. Lake Harbor	47.	d. Temple of Serapis
43.	e. Lighthouse	48.	e. Western Harbor

VI Directions

Match the definition to its character.

49. puer Aegyptius   a. pharum ingentem habuit.

50. Alexandria   b. faber Graecus erat.

51. Barbillus   c. erat servus quem Aegyptii interfecerunt.

52. Diogenes   d. erat vir qui numquam tacet.

53. Plancus   e. cum Caecilio negotium egit.

VII Directions

Select the answers that most correctly complete the following culture statements.

54. **Select what was <u>not a reason</u> for founding Alexandria at its present site.**
    a. the Lighthouse   b. good harbor   c. fresh water

55. **The major activities that made Alexandria important were _____.**
    a. fighting and sailing
    b. trade and education
    c. slave trading and glassmaking

56. **The characteristics of the Ancient Wonder of the World found in Alexandria were that it _____.**
    a. was 100 ft. wide and made of marble
    b. was lit continuously day and night and was over 400 ft. tall
    c. had a one-half million volume library and sculpture gallery

57. **The Museum contained _____.**
    a. a continuously burning fire
    b. a one-half million volume library
    c. a tremendous cult statue

58. **The most powerful people in Alexandria were the _____.**
    a. Romans   b. Egyptians   c. Greeks

59. **An advantage this group did <u>not</u> enjoy was _____.**
    a. the official language
    b. wealth
    c. the largest number in population

60. **Alexandria was known world wide for the peaceful relations displayed by its numerous inhabitants.**
    a. True   b. False

VIII Directions

Select the form of the word which makes the sentence correct.

61. **The merchants were walking through the city.**
    mercatores per _____ ambulabant.
    a. urbi   b. urbem   c. urbes   d. urbium

62. **He always wants to chatter about the temples of Alexandria.**
    semper de _____ Alexandriae garrire vult.
    a. templo   b. templa   c. templorum   d. templis

63. **The merchant was alone in the desert, without water.**
    mercator erat solus in desertis, sine _____.
    a. aquis   b. aqua   c. aquam   d. aquae

64. **The man had bought these gems from a merchant.**
    vir has gemmas a _____ emerat.
    a. mercatori   b. mercatore   c. mercatorem   d. mercatores

65. **The thieves rushed into the house of the craftsman.**
    latrones in _____ fabri ruerunt.
    a. casae   b. casam   c. casa   d. casarum

IX   Directions

Match the Latin word to its antonym/opposite.

66. difficilis   a. numquam

67. multi   b. discedo

68. semper   c. sine

69. cum   d. facilis

70. appropinquo   e. pauci

X   Directions

Match each of the following quotations to a picture below.

    a. postquam ad aram venit, ibi vinum fudit.
    b. multi homines in viis Alexandriae stant.
    c. navis facile ad portum pervenit quod pharum habuit.
    d. facile erat Barbillo servum Quinto dare quod multos servos habebat.
    e. Quintus facile villam splendidam Barbilli invenire poterat.

71.

72.

73.

74.

75.

XI Directions

Identify the case of the underlined word.

76. **ad portum <u>Alexandriae</u> mox pervenimus.**
    a. nominative   b. genitive   c. dative   d. accusative   e. ablative

77. **in villa Barbilli erant multi <u>servi</u>.**
    a. nominative   b. genitive   c. dative   d. accusative   e. ablative

78. **oculi monstri <u>flammas</u> emittebant.**
    a. nominative   b. genitive   c. dative   d. accusative   e. ablative

79. **pro <u>multitudine</u> Aegyptiorum erat senex.**
    a. nominative   b. genitive   c. dative   d. accusative   e. ablative

80. **Barbillus <u>mihi</u> multas gemmas ostendit.**
    a. nominative   b. genitive   c. dative   d. accusative   e. ablative

XII Directions

Select the English sentence that correctly translates the Latin sentence.

81. **ad portum Athenarum mox pervenimus.**
    a. Athens arrived at night at the port.
    b. At night we reached the port of Athens.
    c. We soon arrived at the port of Athens.

82. **fures Romani per vias urbis incedebant.**
    a. The city streets of Rome were filled with thieves.
    b. The Romans were marching through the streets of the city of Rome.
    c. The Roman thieves were marching through the streets of the city.

83. **iuvenes et pueri ad tabernam mercatoris contenderunt.**
    a. The shop of the merchant was near the boys and young men.
    b. The young men and boys hurried to the shop of the merchant.
    c. The young men and merchants hurried to the shop of the boy.

84. **in multitudine Romanorum erat infans.**
    a. Among the Romans there were a lot of children.
    b. In the crowd of Romans was a child.
    c. There was a crowd of Roman children.

85. **omnes nautae pro templo Neptuni stabant.**
    a. The temple of Neptune used to stand near all the ships.
    b. The statues of Neptune are all in front of the temple.
    c. All the sailors were standing in front of the temple of Neptune.

XIII Directions

Match the definition to its culture term.

86. Museum   a. mathematician who wrote a geometry textbook

87. obelisk   b. the university of Alexandria

88. Royal Quarter   c. proposed that the Earth revolved around the Sun

89. Aristarchus   d. granite monument with a pointed top

90. Euclid   e. the square mile containing government buildings, temples, etc.

XIV Directions

Answer the following questions based on your knowledge of Latin vocabulary.

91. Which Latin word does **NOT** refer to time?
     a. diu   b. paulisper   c. huc   d. cotidie   e. mox

92. Which Latin word does **NOT** refer to motion?
     a. debere   b. appropinquare   c. procedere   d. ambulare   e. redire

93. Which Latin word does **NOT** refer to ancient religion?
     a. templum   b. aliquid   c. sacerdos   d. ara   e. victima

94. Which Latin word does **NOT** refer to the sea?
     a. unda   b. litus   c. mare   d. ordo   e. aqua

95. Which Latin word does **NOT** indicate approval or encouragement?
     a. plausus   b. laudare   c. favere   d. incitare   e. invitus

96. Which Latin word would we consider complimentary or positive?
     a. ignavus   b. benignus   c. stultus   d. iratus   e. ferox

XV Directions

Match the Stage 17 Vocabulary Checklist word to the word which means nearly the same.

97. multitudo   a. ingentissimus

98. maximus   b. agmen

99. pervenire   c. turba

100. quondam   d. olim

                     e. appropinquare

Stage 18 Test

PLEASE DO NOT WRITE ON THE TEST BOOKLET.
MARK ALL ANSWERS ON THE ANSWER SHEET.

I Directions

Read the following story.

olim Quintus ad tabernam Clementis contendit. ubi ad tabernam	1
pervenit, Clementem salutavit.	2
"audi, amice," inquit. "ego tibi aliquid dicere volo. ad **pyramides** iter	3
facere cupio. sunt enim in Aegypto multae pyramides quas Aegyptii olim	4
exstruxerunt. Aegyptii in pyramidibus reges **sepelire** solebant. ego	5
pyramides videre volo quod sunt maximae et pulcherrimae. visne	6
mecum iter facere?"	7
Clemens laetus consensit. itaque Quintus et Clemens pecuniam et	8
cibum in **saccis** posuerunt. tum ad Plutum, mercatorem Graecum,	9
festinaverunt et **camelos conduxerunt**. saccos, quos e taberna Clementis	10
portaverant, in camelis posuerunt. tum camelos **conscenderunt** et ex	11
urbe discesserunt. per agros et villas procedebant.	12
subito decem Aegyptii, qui **insidias** paraverant, impetum fecerunt.	13
Quintus et Clemens fortiter resistebant sed facile erat Aegyptiis eos	14
superare quod **fustes** ingentes habebant. tum Aegyptii cum pecunia et	15
camelis effugerunt. Quintus et Clemens **tristes** ad urbem reveniebant.	16
"eheu!" inquit Clemens. "quam miseri sumus! pyramides non	17
vidimus: pecuniam et camelos amisimus."	18

> **Words and Phrases**
>
> **pyramides** - pyramids   **conduxerunt** - rented
> **exstruxerunt** - built   **conscenderunt** - mounted
> **sepelire** - to bury   **insidias** - ambush
> **saccis** - bags   **fustes** - clubs
> **camelos** - camels   **tristes** - sad

II Directions

*Indicate whether the following story statements are true or false by marking **a** for **true** and **b** for **false**.*

1. Clemens came to visit Quintus.

2. Clemens had a suggestion.

3. The plan was to visit the pyramids.

4. The Egyptians used these structures to praise their gods.

5. The speaker especially wanted to see these structures because of their size and age.

6. They prepared for the trip by gathering food and clothes as well as renting camels.

7. The merchant who rented the camels was Egyptian.

8. Our dynamic duo was ambushed by five Egyptian thugs with clubs.

9. Our dynamic duo's efforts to defend themselves from the attack were successful.

10. Clemens complained that nothing had turned out the way they had planned.

III Directions

Identify the following grammar/structure items based on the content of the story.

11. **In line 3 <u>dicere</u> is a _____ conjugation verb.**
   a. first　　　　b. second　　　　c. third　　　　d. fourth

12. **In line 4 the gender and number of <u>quas</u> is _____.**
   a. masc. sing.　b. masc. pl.　　c. fem. sing.　　d. fem. pl.

13. **In line 5 <u>sepelire</u> is a _____ conjugation verb.**
   a. first　　　　b. second　　　　c. third　　　　d. fourth

14. **In line 5 the tense of the verb <u>solebant</u> is _____.**
   a. present　　　b. imperfect　　c. perfect　　　d. pluperfect

15. **In line 6 the translation of <u>quod</u> is _____.**
   a. which　　　　b. what　　　　c. because　　　d. how

16. **In line 6 the degree of the adjective <u>maximae</u> is _____.**
   a. positive　　b. comparative　c. superlative　d. regular

17. **In line 13 the tense of the verb <u>paraverant</u> is _____.**
   a. present　　　b. imperfect　　c. perfect　　　d. pluperfect

18. **In line 14 the case of the word <u>Aegyptiis</u> is _____ .**
    a. nominative   b. accusative   c. dative   d. genitive

19. **In line 17 the translation of the word <u>quam</u> is _____ .**
    a. which   b. what   c. because   d. how

20. **In line 18 the understood subject of <u>amisimus</u> is _____ .**
    a. vos   b. ego   c. nos   d. tu

IV Directions

Select the word(s) that most closely define(s) the <u>underlined</u> derivative.

21. **The soldier was known for his <u>audacious</u> behavior.**
    a. reliable   b. conscientious   c. stupid   d. daring

22. **The general decided that the most effective form of execution was <u>decapitation</u>.**
    a. strangulation   c. chopping off the head
    b. poison   d. firing squad

23. **The soldier was part of a <u>reconnaissance</u> mission.**
    a. food gathering   c. fact finding
    b. terrorist   d. troop gathering

24. **The students sent <u>petitions</u> to the principal.**
    a. requests   b. commands   c. notes   d. gifts

25. **She hesitated to mail the <u>fragile</u> package.**
    a. expensive   b. breakable   c. heavy   d. ancient

26. **Her son had never been <u>demonstrative</u>.**
    a. depressed   b. happy   c. affectionate   d. hot headed

27. **The owl is a <u>nocturnal</u> bird.**
    a. day-loving   b. winter-loving   c. summer-loving   d. night-loving

28. **The officer put him in <u>manacles</u>.**
    a. prison clothes   b. a stockade   c. handcuffs   d. a line-up

29. **The teacher gave <u>partial</u> credit for the answer.**
    a. complete   b. part   c. no   d. extra

30. **Originally that which was <u>profane</u> was done _____ a temple.**

    a. in front of   b. throughout   c. near   d. beyond

V   Directions

Indicate whether the following culture statements are true or false by marking **a** *for* **true** *and* **b** *for* **false.**

31. Casting and core-forming were expensive techniques for making glass.

32. The technique of glassblowing was discovered in Alexandria.

33. The earliest known evidence of glass dates from A.D. 1500.

34. Glass was one of Alexandria's most successful industries.

35. Glass is made of sand and sodium bicarbonate.

36. The evolution of glassmaking went from glazing pottery through formation around a core to glassblowing.

37. The land around Alexandria was fertilized each year by the flooding of the Ocean.

38. The major crop grown in Egypt was wheat.

39. The rulers of Egypt before the Romans were the Greeks.

40. The major agricultural work in Egypt was done by the peasants.

41. The farm workers were grateful for the kindnesses the government showed them.

42. Because taxation was so prevalent in Egypt, bribery of the officials became a very common part of life.

43. The arrival of the Romans marked an improvement in the way Egyptian peasants were treated.

44. Roman emperors kept Egypt under their personal control.

45. Romans in Egypt did not continue the practice of mummification.

VI Directions

Match the definitions to the characters from the stories in Stage 18.

46. Clemens   a. were people who paid extortion money to the villain of the tale.

47. Eutychus   b. helped the hero save the day and hurt Eutychus.

48. feles   c. was a proud follower of Isis who saved the day.

49. Isis   d. owned the largest glass factory in Alexandria.

50. tabernarii   e. was an Egyptian goddess personified by a cat.

****

51. Barbillus   a. was the stubborn freedman of Barbillus.

52. operae   b. owned at least 30 shops in Alexandria.

53. Quintus   c. were the four guards Clemens addressed.

54. senex   d. supported the freedman from Pompeii.

55. servi Aegyptii   e. were thugs.

VII Directions

Identify the declension to which each of the nouns belongs.
*Use **a** for 1st, **b** for 2nd, **c** for 3rd, **d** for 4th, **e** for 5th.*

56. effigiei

57. florum

58. saxi

59. agminum

60. animorum

61. tumultus

62. noctis

63. impetuum

VIII Directions

*Odd One Out. Choose the word which does **NOT** belong in each category.*

64. Which word is **NOT** a fourth declension word?
    a. tumultus   b. portus   c. litus   d. impetus

65. Which word is **NOT** in the accusative case?
    a. agmen   b. noctium   c. effigiem   d. negotium

66. Which word is **NOT** plural?
    a. aedificia   b. itinera   c. litora   d. aula

67. Which word is **NOT** singular?
    a. dona   b. faber   c. vita   d. iter

68. Which word is **NOT** in the genitive case?
    a. rerum   b. manuum   c. auxiliorum   d. aris

69. Which word does **NOT** describe an occupation?
    a. liber   b. faber   c. nauta   d. agricola

70. Which word is **NOT** the name of an Egyptian deity?
    a. Serapis   b. Horus   c. Bastet   d. Plancus

      Stage 18

IX Directions

Select the word that correctly completes the sentence.

71. **On the street of glassmakers there was a huge crowd.**

in via _____ erat ingens turba.
a. vitrearius   b. vitreariorum   c. vitrearium

72. **It is not proper for you to block the freedman.**

non decorum est tibi _____ obstare.
a. libertum   b. liberto   c. libertus

73. **Then Eutychus gave a sign to his thugs.**

tum Eutychus _____ signum dedit.
a. operas   b. operis   c. operarum

74. **In the shop of Clemens were many vases.**

in taberna _____ erant multae ollae.
a. Clementem   b. Clementi   c. Clementis

75. **The Egyptians approached Quintus.**

Aegyptii _____ appropinquaverunt.
a. Quintum   b. Quinti   c. Quinto

76. **Clemens, however, did not trust Eutychus.**

Clemens tamen _____ non credebat.
a. Eutycho   b. Eutychum   c. Eutychi

77. **The freedman was not weak but strong.**

libertus non erat _____ sed fortis.
a. infirmum   b. infirmus   c. infirmi

78. **The old man and his wife were terrified.**

senex et uxor erant _____ .
a. perterritus   b. perterriti   c. perterrita

79. **The priests led Clemens into the sanctuary.**

sacerdotes Clementem in cellam _____ .
a. ducit   b. duxisti   c. duxerunt

80. **The slaves were brandishing huge clubs.**

servi _____ fustes vibrabant.
a. ingens   b. ingentes   c. ingentibus

X Directions

Match the pictures to the glassmaking procedure used to create the item.

A.

B.

C.

D.

81. millefiori

82. core-formed

83. ribbon glass

84. blown glass

XI Directions

Match the Latin word to the word which is most nearly opposite in meaning.

85. dies   a. petere

86. postulare   b. nox

87. effugere   c. discedere

88. advenire   d. consistere

89. invite   e. libenter

XII Directions

Choose the form of the word which makes the sentence correct.

90. **All the shopowners seek help from Eutychus.**
     omnes tabernarii auxilium a _____ petunt.
     a. Eutychi   b. Eutychus   c. Eutychum   d. Eutycho

91. **Cervix used to go to the barns every day.**
    Cervix ad _____ cotidie adibat.
    a. horrea b. horrei   c. horreo   d. horreum

92. **The temple of Isis was near the shop of Clemens.**
    templum Isidis prope _____ Clementis erat.
    a. tabernae b. taberna c. tabernam d. tabernis

93. **In front of Eutychus' shop stood four Egyptian slaves.**
    pro _____ Eutychi stabant quattuor servi Aegyptii.
    a. tabernae b. taberna c. tabernam d. tabernis

XIII Directions

Identify the speakers of the following statements from our stories.

94. _____ inquit, "non decorum est tibi liberto obstare."
    a. Quintus b. Barbillus c. Clemens d. Eutychus

95. _____ inquit, "necesse est ei poenas dare."
    a. Quintus b. Barbillus c. Clemens d. Eutychus

96. _____ inquit, "operae libertum meum interfecerunt."
    a. Quintus b. Barbillus c. Clemens d. Eutychus

XIV Directions

Match the pictures to their Latin descriptions.

A.  B.  C.  D.

97. Clemens feminae ollam ostendit. 99. feles caput Eutychi petivit.

98. feles in taberna vitrearii sedebat. 100. Eutychus et operae vinum bibebant.

Stage 19 Test

PLEASE DO NOT WRITE ON THE TEST BOOKLET.
MARK ALL ANSWERS ON THE ANSWER SHEET.

I Directions

Read this continuation of the Stage 18 Test story.

Quintus et Clemens per urbem fessi procedebant. ubi tabernam Pluti	1
praeteribant, rem mirabilem viderunt. **cameli**, quos Aegyptii **abduxerant,**	2
extra tabernam Pluti stabant! tum Quintus rem totam intellexit. amici irati	3
mercatorem quaesiverunt, sed invenire non poterant. aderat tamen puer	4
parvus qui camelos custodiebat. Quintus puero clamavit,	5
"heus, tu! ubi sunt Aegyptii qui **contra** nos impetum fecerunt? ego eos	6
de pecunia mea **interrogare** volo."	7
puer perterritus, "roga Plutum," inquit, et statim fugit.	8
amici per vias Alexandriae Plutum frustra quaesiverunt. tandem	9
thermas intraverunt. ecce! Plutus in palaestra **duobus** cum servis	10
ambulabat. Quintus servos agnovit. eos enim viderat in turba	11
Aegyptiorum qui impetum fecerant. Quintus ad Plutum processit, qui,	12
postquam eum iratum vidit, valde timebat. e sella celeriter surrexit.	13
Quintus clamavit,	14
"ubi est mea pecunia? camelos iam invenimus!"	15
Plutus erat perterritus quod Quintus erat civis Romanus. Plutus Quinto	16
"**ignosce** mihi," inquit. "ego tibi pecuniam libenter reddo et parvum	17
donum tibi offero."	18
deinde Quintum et Clementem ad villam suam duxit. ibi eis duos	19
equos dedit. Quintus numquam equos pulchriores quam illos viderat!	20
tum Quintus et Clemens equos **conscenderunt** et ad **pyramides** laeti	21
contenderunt.	22

Words and Phrases

praeteribant - pass by	**interrogare** - to ask
cameli - camels	**duobus** - two
abduxerant - had stolen	**ignosce** - forgive
extra - outside of	**conscenderunt** - mounted
contra - against	**pyramides** - pyramids

II Directions

Indicate whether the following comprehension statements are true or false by marking **a** *for* **true** *and* **b** *for* **false.**

1. Quintus and Clemens were quickly returning to the city.

2. They saw their camels inside Plutus' shop.

3. Quintus first questioned Plutus about the camels.

4. Quintus wanted to question the Egyptians who had made an attack on Clemens and him.

5. Quintus found Plutus in the theater with two slaves.

6. The slaves with Plutus had made the attack on Quintus and Clemens.

7. Plutus acted arrogantly around Quintus.

8. Plutus offered to give Quintus his money back and a small gift.

9. Quintus had never seen more beautiful horses than the ones Plutus gave him.

10. Quintus and Clemens were able to visit the pyramids thanks to Plutus' gift.

III Directions

Identify the following grammar/structure items based on the content of the story.

11. **In line 2 <u>viderunt</u> is in the _____ tense.**
    a. present   b. imperfect   c. perfect   d. pluperfect

12. **In line 2 the antecedent of <u>quos</u> is _____.**
    a. cameli   b. Aegyptii   c. tabernam   d. Pluti

13. **In line 4 <u>invenire</u> is a _____ conjugation verb.**
    a. first   b. second   c. third   d. fourth

14. **In line 4 invenire is used as a(n) _____.**
   a. complementary infinitive
   c. subject infinitive
   b. imperative
   d. direct object

15. **In line 9 the case of Alexandriae is _____.**
   a. nominative   b. accusative   c. dative   d. genitive

16. **In line 16 civis is used as a _____.**
   a. subject
   c. direct object
   b. predicate nominative
   d. predicate adjective

17. **In line 17 mihi is used as a(n) _____.**
   a. direct object
   c. indirect object
   b. object of a special verb
   d. possession

18. **In line 17 tibi is used as a(n) _____.**
   a. direct object
   c. indirect object
   b. object of a special verb
   d. possession

19. **In line 20 pulchriores is a _____ adjective.**
   a. positive   b. comparative   c. superlative

20. **In line 21 laeti modifies _____.**
   a. Quintus et Clemens   b. equos   c. pyramides   d. villam

IV Directions

Select the word that correctly completes the sentence.

21. **discipuli, _____!**   a. tace   b. tacete

22. **omnes, _____ vestros vicinos!**   a. ama   b. amate

23. **canis, _____!**   a. sede   b. sedete

24. **poetae, _____!**   a. noli recitare b. nolite recitare

25. **fili, _____!**   a. surge   b. surgite

26. _____ , aperi ianuam!   a. serve   b. servus

27. _____ , cur fenestras clausisti?   a. ancilla   b. ancillae

28. _____ , nolite discedere!   a. femina   b. feminae

29. _____ , curre!   a. latro   b. latrones

30. _____ , bibe vinum!   a. mercator   b. mercatores

V Directions

Select the word(s) that correctly define(s) the underlined derivative.

31. **The injury was extremely vexatious.**
    a. long-lasting   b. annoying   c. painful   d. minor

32. **A vacation often has a curative effect.**
    a. harmful   b. depressing   c. gentle   d. healing

33. **The teacher was very vivacious.**
    a. well-mannered b. lively   c. good-looking d. talkative

34. **The sudden rise in the cost of fuel oil brought vociferous protests from all.**
    a. straightforward b. noisy   c. severe   d. written

35. **Spectacular results were produced by the itinerant salesman.**
    a. laughing   b. talkative   c. traveling   d. good-looking

36. **The theme of the President's speech was amity.**
    a. hope   b. friendship   c. pleasure   d. pity

37. **The climbers followed a perilous route up the Matterhorn.**
    a. dangerous   b. steep   c. easy   d. beautiful

38. **The castigation of the accused was penalty enough.**
    a. banishment   b. financial ruin c. arrest   d. severe criticism

39. **He was negligent in picking up his girlfriend on time.**
    a. prompt   b. careless   c. eager   d. tardy

40. **The dulcet strains of Orpheus' lyre soothed Cerberus.**
    a. sweet-sounding b. muffled   c. quavering   d. harsh

VI Directions

Select the adjective that most correctly completes the sentence.

41. _____ femina est Galatea, mater Helenae.

   a. hoc   b. hic   c. haec

42. _____ horrea sunt maxima.

   a. hi   b. hae   c. haec

43. iuvenes _____ puellas spectant.

   a. hos   b. has   c. haec

44. _____ vir tragoedias scribere non potest.

   a. hic   b. haec   c. hoc

45. _____ sacerdotes sacrificium faciunt.

   a. hae   b. hi   c. haec

46. Aristo _____ amicos non amat.

   a. hos   b. has   c. haec

47. _____ rosae erant pulchrae.

   a. hae   b. hi   c. haec

48. Helena _____ virum iterum agitat.

   a. hanc   b. hunc   c. hoc

49. puer _____ puellam non delectat.

   a. haec   b. hae   c. hanc

50. _____ templum est magnificum.

   a. hic   b. hunc   c. hoc

VII Directions

Match the Latin word to its antonym/opposite.

51. paucissimi   a. castigavi

52. coepi   b. filiae

53. laudavi   c. plurimi

54. sonitus   d. confeci

55. filii   e. silentium

VIII Directions

*Select the word which does **NOT** belong in each group.*

56. Which word does **NOT** pertain to a family member?
    a. mater   b. filia   c. familiaris   d. portus   e. pater

57. Which word is **NOT** a body part?
    a. praesidium   b. pes   c. caput   d. manus   e. umerus

58. Which word does **NOT** describe a negative action?
    a. castigare   b. punire   c. cogitare   d. vexare   e. deridere

59. Which word is **NOT** related to sound?
    a. audire   b. vox   c. sonitus   d. clamare   e. tenere

IX Directions

*Indicate whether the following culture statements are true or false by marking **a** for **true** and **b** for **false**.*

60. The Roman name for Horus was Serapis.

61. The festival of Isis was always held on April 5th.

62. The worship of Isis was found in Egypt and other countries.

63. Isis was not very well-respected by the Egyptians.

64. One major belief of Isis worship was that she offered the hope of life after death.

65. Isis was believed to be responsible for new life in the spring.

66. The festival of Isis marked the beginning of hunting season.

67. The <u>pompa</u> was very noisy.

68. The procession carried the statue of Isis down to the Great Harbor.

69. Every year a new boat loaded with spices and flowers was sent out to sea with the statue of the goddess on it.

70. The initiation ceremony for the cult of Isis was well-known to everyone.

X   Directions

Select the word that correctly completes the sentence.

71. cur _____ feminam vituperas?   a. illum   b. illam   c. illud

72. _____ donum est splendidum.   a. illam   b. illud   c. illum

73. _____ iuvenis est optimus.   a. ille   b. illi   c. illae

74. duo iuvenes, _____ Galatea emoverat,   a. qui   b. quos   c. quem
    pompam non viderunt.

75. Isis, _____ sistrum tenebat,   a. quod   b. quae   c. qui
    stolam croceam gerebat.

XI   Directions

Match the definition to the noun(s).

76. Aristo   a. was the son of an Egyptian god who had been killed.

77. Isiaci   b. was the tragedy writer whose life was a tragedy.

78. Galatea   c. was the crabby wife who scolded her husband.

79. Helena   d. was the daughter who attracted men.

80. Horus   e. were the followers of the deity worshiped by Clemens.

81.	cella	a.	was the deity worshiped by Clemens.
82.	Isis	b.	was the sacred rattle of Isis.
83.	Osiris	c.	was the inner sanctuary of a temple.
84.	sistrum	d.	was the husband who was brought back to life.
85.	*The Golden Ass*	e.	was a novel describing the preparations of one planning to become a follower of Isis.

XII Directions

Identify the following noun forms as either **nominative** *case,* **vocative** *case, or* **both** **nominative** *and* **vocative** *case.*

Use **a** = *nominative case only*
   b = *both nominative and vocative case*
   c = *vocative case only*

86.	Eutyche	90.	filii
87.	Barbillus	91.	puer
88.	custodes	92.	nautae
89.	Caecilii		

XIII Directions

Identify the following verb forms as **imperatives** *or* **infinitives.** *Use*

a = *positive singular imperative*   **d** = *negative singular imperative*
b = *positive plural imperative*   **e** = *negative plural imperative*
c = *infinitive*

93.	nolite currere	97.	doce
94.	da	98.	noli trahere
95.	audite	99.	docere
96.	esse	100.	ferte

Stage 20 Test

PLEASE DO NOT WRITE ON THE TEST BOOKLET.
MARK ALL ANSWERS ON THE ANSWER SHEET.

I   Directions

Read the following story.

omnes tacuerunt et Petronem intente audiverunt.	1
"Barbillus Aristoni nullam pecuniam reliquit," inquit Petro, "sed	2
tragoedias, quas Aristo scripserat, reddidit."	3
amici statim riserunt quod tragoediae Aristonis pessimae erant.	4
Galatea quoque risit.	5
"decorum est Barbillo nullam pecuniam Aristoni relinquere," inquit	6
Galatea. "Barbillus Aristoni tragoedias **solum** reliquit quod Aristo nihil	7
aliud curat. **sine dubio** Barbillus mihi multam pecuniam reliquit quod	8
ego **prudentior** sum quam maritus meus."	9
tum Petro Galateae dixit, "Barbillus filiae tuae gemmas, quas a	10
mercatore Arabi emit, reliquit."	11
"quam fortunata est Helena!" exclamaverunt amici.	12
Galatea hanc rem graviter ferebat.	13
"non decorum est Helenae gemmas habere. nam Helena est stultior	14
quam pater. **tutius est** Helenae gemmas mihi tradere. sed cur nihil de me	15
dicis, Petro? quid Barbillus mihi reliquit?"	16
Petro tamen nihil respondit.	17
"dic mihi, stultissime," inquit Galatea irata.	18
tandem Petro **susurravit**, "nihil tibi reliquit."	19
omnes amici valde commoti erant: multi cachinnaverunt, pauci	20
lacrimaverunt.	21
Galatea tamen tacebat. **humi** deciderat exanimata.	22

Words and Phrases	
solum - only	**tutius est** - it is safer
sine dubio - without a doubt	**susurravit** - whispered
prudentior - more prudent	**humi** - on the ground

II Directions

Indicate whether the following comprehension statements are true or false by marking **a** *for* **true** *and* **b** *for* **false**.

1. All the people told Petro to be quiet and to listen to them.

2. Aristo received nothing from the will.

3. His friends were upset about this result.

4. Galatea approved of the situation.

5. Galatea assumes that Aristo cares for nothing else.

6. Galatea felt that she should get a lot of money because she was more beautiful than her husband.

7. Their friends described Helena as fortunate because Barbillus had left her the Arabian gems.

8. Galatea thought that Helena's inheritance was fair.

9. Galatea assumed that she could take better care of Barbillus' gift than her daughter could.

10. Petro said many things about what Galatea received in the will.

11. Galatea's reaction to her inheritance was laughter.

III Directions

Identify the following grammar/structure items based on the content of the story.

12. **In line 2 <u>Aristoni</u> is in the _____ case.**
    a. nominative   b. genitive   c. dative   d. accusative

13. **In line 2 <u>Aristoni</u> is used as a(n) _____.**
    a. subject   c. indirect object
    b. direct object   d. object of a special verb

14. **In line 3 <u>scripserat</u> is in the _____ tense.**
    a. present   b. imperfect   c. perfect   d. pluperfect

15. **In line 4 <u>pessimae</u> is a _____ adjective.**
    a. positive   b. comparative   c. superlative

16. **In line 6 <u>Aristoni</u> is used as a(n)** _____.
   a. direct object   c. indirect object
   b. object of a special verb   d. adjective

17. **In line 9 <u>quam</u> is translated as** _____.
   a. how   b. than   c. which

18. **In line 10 <u>quas</u> is translated as** _____.
   a. how   b. than   c. which

19. **In line 12 <u>quam</u> is translated as** _____.
   a. how   b. than   c. which

20. **In line 18 <u>stultissime</u> is in the** _____ **case.**
   a. nominative   c. accusative
   b. vocative   d. dative

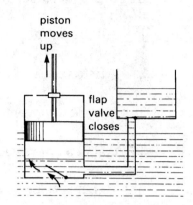

piston moves up

flap valve closes

IV   Directions

Match the definitions to the English derivatives.

21. auricle   a. place of residence

22. artifact   b. to shame "to death"

23. domicile   c. external part of the ear

24. lunacy   d. object made by human hands

25. mortify   e. intermittent insanity caused by the phases of the moon

****

26. artisan   a. person between the ages of 40 to 50

27. doctrine   b. having 20 angles

28. lunate   c. something taught

29. quadragenarian   d. skilled workman

30. vigintiangular   e. crescent-shaped

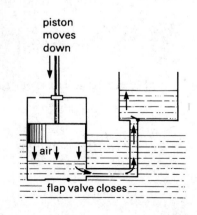

piston moves down

air

flap valve closes

Directions

Select the correct answer for these Latin math problems.

31. **viginti plus triginta**
    a. quinquaginta   b. quadraginta   c. triginta

32. **quinquaginta minus decem**
    a. quinquaginta   b. quadraginta   c. triginta

33. **decem plus viginti**
    a. quinquaginta   b. quadraginta   c. triginta

34. **triginta minus duodeviginti**
    a. duodecim   b. undecim   c. decem

35. **undecim plus octo**
    a. viginti   b. duodeviginti   c. undeviginti

36. **novem minus duo**
    a. undecim   b. decem   c. septem

37. **octo plus decem minus quinque**
    a. septem   b. tredecim   c. tres

38. **sex minus tres plus tredecim**
    a. sedecim   b. quattuor   c. quattuordecim

39. **quattuor plus tres plus tredecim**
    a. quattuordecim   b. duodecim   c. viginti

40. **quinquaginta minus quadraginta plus quinque**
    a. quinque   b. quindecim   c. triginta

VI Directions

Name the Alexandrian scientist associated with the device or experiment found in each picture.

41.

    a. Hero   b. Hippocrates   c. Euclid   d. Eratosthenes

42.

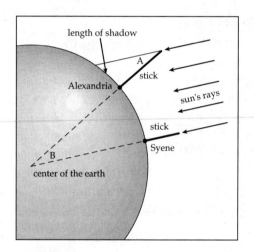

    a. Copernicus   b. Eratosthenes   c. Aristarchus   d. Ptolemy

VII Directions

Match the definition to the scientist.

43. Copernicus   a. was the most famous Alexandrian anatomist.

44. Eratosthenes   b. was the Alexandrian mathematician known for his work, *Elements*.

45. Euclid   c. was the father of medical science.

46. Herophilus   d. was the Renaissance scientist who "rediscovered" that the Earth circled the Sun.

47. Hippocrates   e. was the Greek who calculated the circumference of the Earth.

VIII Directions

Match the definition to the story character.

48. astrologus   a. erat amicus Rufi qui medicus erat in Graecia. Rufum ad nuptias invitavit.

49. Barbillus   b. in Aegypto habitavit. erat amicus Caecilii et amicus Quinti et Clementis.

50. Eupor   c. hic homo in villa Barbilli habitabat. dominum interfecit.

51. Galatea   d. erat femina quae maritum semper castigabat.

****

52. Petro   a. uxor Barbilli erat femina placida quae in naufragio mortua est.

53. Plotina   b. multos sermones cum Barbillo vulnerato habebat. tabernam liberto dedit.

54. Quintus   c. erat filius Barbilli. pater eum ire ad Graeciam noluit, sed is cum matre iit.

55. Rufus   d. hic medicus Graecus Barbillum sanare temptavit.

IX Directions

*Choose the correct translation of the forms of the **personal pronoun.***

56. Clemens officinam Eutychi intravit. Eutychus **eum** salutavit.
    a. he   b. his   c. him

57. operae celeriter convenerunt. Eutychus **eis** fustes tradidit.
    a. to them   b. their   c. they

58. Helena nos ad cenam invitavit. nos ad villam **eius** festinavimus.
    a. she   b. her   c. they

59. servi celeriter adibant. vilicus **eos** vehementer laudavit.
    a. they   b. them   c. their

60. Phormio culinam intravit. vilicus **eam** inspexit.
    a. her   b. him   c. it

61. ancillae culinam intraverunt. **eae** coquum salutaverunt.
   a. she   b. they   c. to her

62. Quintus multa templa in urbe vidit. iuvenis **ea** laudavit.
   a. she   b. they   c. them

63. Helena diem natalem celebrabat. pater **ei** gemmam dedit.
   a. she   b. they   c. to her

X   Directions

Indicate whether the following culture statements are true or false by marking **a** *for* **true** *and* **b** *for* **false**.

64. The Roman contribution to health was in the field of public sanitation.

65. Epidermis wrote a book on medicine and surgery, i.e. how to remove tonsils, decayed teeth.

66. The Egyptians believed in studying only the outside of the body to search for the causes of disease.

67. The Greeks were very fond of dissecting a body for medical study.

68. The most important part of Alexandrian medicine was the stress it placed on hygiene, diet, exercise, and bathing.

69. Some very successful treatments were the juice of the wild poppy to relieve pain and the use of unwashed wool to help with swelling.

70. Astronomy originated at the university in Alexandria.

71. Major improvements over the quality of ancient medicine came about only 150 years ago in Europe.

72. Alexandrians put all of their scientific inventions to work in industry.

73. The great reliance on slave labor greatly limited the use of Alexandrian inventions.

74. The Hippocratic Oath makes inventors swear to a high standard of conduct.

75. The doctor's use of cobwebs on Barbillus' wound was a totally useless procedure.

XI Directions

Based on the pictures, select the correct form of the present participle to complete the sentences.

76. **videsne servos _____ Barbillum?**

    a. portans   b. portantem   c. portantes

77. **hae ancillae, prope lectum _____ , dominum spectabant.**

    a. stans   b. stantem   c. stantes

78. **astrologum _____ in cubiculum videmus.**

    a. irrumpens   b. irrumpentem   c. irrumpentes

79. **Quintus Barbillum _____ videt.**

    a. recumbens   b. recumbentem   c. recumbentes

80. **Phormio, ad urbem _____ , medicum quaerit.**

    a. currens   b. currentem   c. currentes

XII Directions

Select the word that most correctly completes the following grammar/structure items.

in media officina Eutychum vinum bibentem vidimus.

81. Identify the <u>participle</u> in the sentence.
    a. media   b. vinum   c. bibentem

82. Identify the word the <u>participle modifies</u>.
    a. officina   b. Eutychum   c. vinum

83. Identify the <u>number</u> of the participle.
    a. singular   b. plural

XIII Directions

Select the English sentence that correctly translates the Latin sentence.

84. **Aegyptii, extra tabernam stantes, Quintum viderunt.**
    a. The Egyptians saw Quintus standing outside of the shop.
    b. The Egyptians, standing outside of the shop, saw Quintus.
    c. The Egyptian, standing outside of the shop, saw Quintus.

85. **flumen Nilus, per praedium Barbilli fluens, erat pulcherrimum.**
    a. The Nile River, flowing through the estate of Barbillus, is very beautiful.
    b. The Nile River, flowing through the estate of Barbillus, was beautiful.
    c. The Nile River, flowing through the estate of Barbillus, was very beautiful.

86. **Phormio medicum, per forum ambulantem, conspexit.**
    a. Phormio, walking through the forum, caught sight of the doctor.
    b. Phormio caught sight of the doctor walking through the forum.
    c. The doctor, walking with Phormio, caught sight of the forum.

XIV Directions

Match the definition to the term.

87. remedium astrologi   a. peppercorn and lanolin

88. remedium Phormionis   b. a black mouse

89. remedium Petronis   c. spiders' webs

                                d. vinegar, sutures, and rest

XV Directions

Match the Latin word to the word which means approximately the same.

90. adire

91. collocare

92. doctus

a. callidus

b. appropinquare

c. ignavus

d. ponere

XVI Directions

Match the Latin word to its antonym/opposite.

93. crudelis

94. arcessere

95. mors

96. pessimus

97. doctus

a. dimittere

b. vita

c. benignus

d. stultus

e. optimus

XVII Directions

Select the word which correctly defines the <u>underlined</u> word.

98. **The astrologer's arguments were very <u>persuasive</u>.**
    a. convincing   b. interesting   c. amusing

99. **Petro's prognosis was uncharacteristically <u>pessimistic</u>.**
    a. gloomy   b. annoying   c. positive

100. **The astrologer did not want to <u>relinquish</u> his influence over Barbillus.**
    a. enjoy   b. give up   c. share

Answers to the Stage Tests

Unit 2 - Stage 13 Test Key

1. c	26. c	51. a	76. a
2. b	27. b	52. a	77. d
3. a	28. d	53. b	78. b
4. c	29. b	54. d	79. e
5. b	30. a	55. d	80. c
6. a	31. b	56. c	81. d
7. a	32. a	57. c	82. a
8. b	33. c	58. a	83. a
9. c	34. e	59. e	84. a
10. b	35. d	60. b	85. a
11. c	36. a	61. d	86. a
12. b	37. d	62. a	87. b
13. a	38. c	63. a	88. a
14. b	39. a	64. c	89. a
15. c	40. b	65. a	90. b
16. b	41. d	66. b	91. a
17. d	42. a	67. a	92. a
18. a	43. c	68. a	93. b
19. c	44. b	69. c	94. c
20. e	45. c	70. c	95. d
21. c	46. b	71. b	96. c
22. e	47. c	72. b	97. b
23. b	48. d	73. d	98. b
24. a	49. c	74. e	99. a
25. d	50. d	75. a	100. b

Unit 2 - Stage 14 Test Key

1. c	26. a	51. c	76. c
2. a	27. b	52. b	77. c
3. b	28. c	53. c	78. b
4. c	29. b	54. a	79. c
5. a	30. c	55. a	80. d
6. c	31. a	56. b	81. e
7. b	32. b	57. a	82. d
8. c	33. c	58. b	83. a
9. b	34. b	59. b	84. c
10. c	35. b	60. a	85. b
11. c	36. a	61. d	86. a
12. b	37. b	62. d	87. c
13. a	38. a	63. d	88. b
14. b	39. c	64. a	89. d
15. b	40. d	65. a	90. d
16. b	41. d	66. d	91. a
17. c	42. c	67. c	92. b
18. a	43. a	68. a	93. d
19. b	44. d	69. d	94. a
20. b	45. c	70. b	95. b
21. d	46. a	71. d	96. a
22. a	47. b	72. c	97. a
23. c	48. a	73. b	98. a
24. b	49. a	74. d	99. b
25. d	50. b	75. a	100. a

Unit 2 - Stage 15 Test Key

1. a	26. c	51. a	76. a
2. b	27. b	52. c	77. b
3. b	28. b	53. d	78. b
4. a	29. b	54. d	79. a
5. b	30. a	55. c	80. e
6. b	31. a	56. c	81. e
7. a	32. c	57. a	82. b
8. a	33. b	58. b	83. c
9. b	34. c	59. a	84. b
10. b	35. d	60. b	85. b
11. a	36. d	61. d	86. a
12. a	37. c	62. d	87. b
13. b	38. a	63. b	88. a
14. b	39. b	64. a	89. b
15. a	40. b	65. c	90. b
16. b	41. a	66. a	91. b
17. b	42. a	67. b	92. b
18. a	43. b	68. b	93. b
19. c	44. a	69. c	94. d
20. c	45. b	70. a	95. c
21. b	46. a	71. a	96. d
22. c	47. a	72. b	97. c
23. a	48. a	73. b	98. a
24. b	49. a	74. b	99. a
25. a	50. b	75. a	100. b

Unit 2 - Stage 16 Test Key

1. c	26. c	51. d	76. a
2. b	27. d	52. a	77. b
3. a	28. c	53. d	78. d
4. b	29. d	54. a	79. a
5. c	30. b	55. c	80. b
6. c	31. c	56. a	81. d
7. c	32. a	57. c	82. a
8. a	33. b	58. d	83. c
9. c	34. c	59. e	84. b
10. b	35. d	60. b	85. c
11. c	36. a	61. e	86. c
12. b	37. d	62. d	87. c
13. a	38. c	63. a	88. b
14. c	39. e	64. c	89. b
15. a	40. a	65. b	90. b
16. a	41. d	66. b	91. d
17. c	42. b	67. d	92. c
18. c	43. a	68. a	93. d
19. a	44. b	69. c	94. a
20. c	45. b	70. c	95. b
21. b	46. a	71. d	96. c
22. c	47. b	72. d	97. b
23. b	48. b	73. b	98. e
24. a	49. a	74. c	99. b
25. d	50. b	75. b	100. e

Unit 2 - Stage 17 Test Key

1. c	26. c	51. e	76. b
2. b	27. d	52. b	77. a
3. b	28. c	53. d	78. d
4. b	29. a	54. a	79. e
5. c	30. a	55. b	80. c
6. c	31. a	56. b	81. c
7. a	32. b	57. b	82. c
8. a	33. a	58. c	83. b
9. b	34. a	59. c	84. b
10. b	35. a	60. b	85. c
11. d	36. b	61. b	86. b
12. b	37. b	62. d	87. d
13. c	38. b	63. b	88. e
14. c	39. b	64. b	89. c
15. a	40. e	65. b	90. a
16. b	41. d	66. d	91. c
17. d	42. a	67. e	92. a
18. a	43. c	68. a	93. b
19. b	44. b	69. c	94. d
20. d	45. e	70. b	95. e
21. b	46. a	71. d	96. b
22. c	47. d	72. c	97. c
23. c	48. c	73. e	98. a
24. d	49. c	74. a	99. e
25. a	50. a	75. b	100. d

Unit 2 - Stage 18 Test Key

1. b	26. c	51. b	76. a
2. b	27. d	52. e	77. b
3. a	28. c	53. d	78. b
4. b	29. b	54. a	79. c
5. b	30. a	55. c	80. b
6. b	31. a	56. e	81. b
7. b	32. b	57. c	82. c
8. b	33. b	58. b	83. a
9. b	34. a	59. c	84. d
10. a	35. b	60. b	85. b
11. c	36. a	61. d	86. a
12. d	37. b	62. c	87. d
13. d	38. a	63. d	88. c
14. b	39. a	64. c	89. e
15. c	40. a	65. b	90. d
16. c	41. b	66. d	91. a
17. d	42. a	67. a	92. c
18. c	43. b	68. d	93. b
19. d	44. a	69. a	94. c
20. c	45. b	70. d	95. d
21. d	46. c	71. b	96. b
22. c	47. d	72. b	97. b
23. c	48. b	73. b	98. c
24. a	49. e	74. c	99. a
25. b	50. a	75. c	100. d

Unit 2 - Stage 19 Test Key

1. b	26. a	51. c	76. b
2. b	27. a	52. d	77. e
3. b	28. b	53. a	78. c
4. a	29. a	54. e	79. d
5. b	30. a	55. b	80. a
6. a	31. b	56. d	81. c
7. b	32. d	57. a	82. a
8. a	33. b	58. c	83. d
9. a	34. b	59. e	84. b
10. a	35. c	60. b	85. e
11. c	36. b	61. b	86. c
12. a	37. a	62. a	87. a
13. d	38. d	63. b	88. b
14. a	39. b	64. a	89. c
15. d	40. a	65. a	90. c
16. b	41. c	66. b	91. b
17. b	42. c	67. a	92. b
18. c	43. b	68. a	93. e
19. b	44. a	69. b	94. a
20. a	45. b	70. b	95. b
21. b	46. a	71. b	96. c
22. b	47. a	72. b	97. a
23. a	48. b	73. a	98. d
24. b	49. c	74. b	99. c
25. a	50. c	75. b	100. b

Unit 2 - Stage 20 Test Key

1. b	26. d	51. d	76. c
2. b	27. c	52. d	77. c
3. b	28. e	53. a	78. b
4. a	29. a	54. b	79. b
5. a	30. b	55. c	80. a
6. b	31. a	56. c	81. c
7. a	32. b	57. a	82. b
8. b	33. c	58. b	83. a
9. a	34. a	59. b	84. b
10. b	35. c	60. c	85. c
11. b	36. c	61. b	86. b
12. c	37. b	62. c	87. b
13. c	38. a	63. c	88. c
14. d	39. c	64. a	89. d
15. c	40. b	65. b	90. b
16. c	41. a	66. b	91. d
17. b	42. b	67. b	92. a
18. c	43. d	68. a	93. c
19. a	44. e	69. a	94. a
20. b	45. b	70. b	95. b
21. c	46. a	71. a	96. e
22. d	47. c	72. b	97. d
23. a	48. c	73. a	98. a
24. e	49. b	74. b	99. a
25. b	50. a	75. b	100. b